What's Really Going ON?

A Collection of Cognitive Restructuring and Resocialization Articles written by Anneshia Freeman for her column entitled "What's Really Going On" featured in the Grand Rapids Times Newspaper

The Grand Master's Keys Publishing – Grand Rapids, MI

Table of Contents

What Do You Define As Real – Matrix I.............................1

The Blind Mind Syndrome – Matrix II.................................5

This Is A Training Simulation – Matrix III..........................10

Who Are the Agents – Matrix IV....................................15

Residual Self-Image – Matrix V.......................................21

Focus is a Weapon – Matrix VI..26

Stop Trying to Hit It…And Hit It – Matrix VII....................32

Downloading – Accessing the Mainframe – Matrix VIII...........37

Unlearning What is Untrue..43

Pick Your Pain...47

What Type of Esteem Do You Have..................................51

What Other People Think – OPP.....................................54

Putting Unrealistic Expectations on Ourselves and Others..........58

Was It the Trap or the Cheese – What's Your Cheese...............65

Unspoken Lies = Articulated Invalidation............................71

The Trust Factor...77

The "Land of Should" Versus the "Is Case"........................82

A Place Called Go...86

The Comfort Zone..90

This Is Nothing..93

They Made That Up – Let's Make Something Else Up.............99

The Non-Negotiable Goal..102

The "I Do That Too" Principle...108

Some the Negation of All..112

My Issues Make My Budget and My Schedule........................117

Finish Strong – The Homestretch..120

My Purpose – My Pain..124

Other Sheep – Not of This Fold...129

Learning the Hard Way – Is That Really Necessary...............136

Why Are You So Fearful...140

Our Father...The Missing File..145

References...153

Acknowledgements

I would like to express my deepest gratitude to the many people who have helped me along my life's journey. Although I will not identify everyone by name, I would like to thank a few who have played a role in my illumination process that has resulted in this book and other books that will follow.

I would like to thank the Woodward Avenue crew in Detroit who introduced me to the slang term "What's Really Going," which I will define in the introduction. I would like to thank Dr. Rhawn Joseph and Dr. Ed Smith for opening my eyes to the power of the unconscious mind. I would also like to thank the following people whose wisdom, wit, knowledge, charm, kindness, and insight have played a crucial role in my personal development: Dr. Patricia Pulliam, Honorable Reverend George K. Heartwell, Helen Cole-Mickens, Marla Edwards, Janell and Tiara Freeman, Eric Thomas, and Carol Chehade. I would like to thank the following organizations and institutes of higher learning: Arbor

Circle Corporation, Black Women's Roundtable, 61st District Court, Grand Rapids Community College, Davenport University, Cornerstone University, and Grand Valley State University.

I would also like to thank my spiritual advisors the late Bishop William C. Abney, Pastor and Lady Jathan Austin, and my current pastors Joel and Yvonne Brooks Junior for their leadership and guidance. I would also like to thank Bishop Noel Jones, Joyce Meyer, and Bishop T.D. Jakes whose mentorship via books, CDs, and DVDs nourished and sustained me during my journey in the wilderness.

Forward

Many people are assigned labels such as healthy, sick, saint, and sinner by others who wear labels such as therapist, minister, doctor, and teacher. In the words of the Roman poet, Juvenal, who warned, “Quis custodiet ipsos custodes?” Translated this means, "Who watches the watchmen?" Well, Anneshia Freeman’s book, **“**What's Really Going on!" embarks on a soul-defining journey to answer this very obstinate question.

Freeman turns the fictionalized film, *The Matrix*, into a series of non-fiction scenarios that make the film seem closer to our current state of reality than we would like to admit. Freeman turns her analysis into a truth table played on the chessboard of life. The very concept of reality is analyzed for validity, as truth must first and foremost stand up to limitless realities. Given this definition, many of the realities that Freeman engages through critical analysis are revealed by their own lack of legitimacy, thus making them deceptions.

Like all revolutionary thinkers, Freeman believes the most revolutionary thing one can do is change self. Some of the chapters like "Residual Self-Image" and "Unlearning What is Untrue" challenge the notions of how individuals tend to define self-identity according to projections of a damaged point of reference that is further sanctioned by an even more wounded society. Thus, insanity is deepened when the macro becomes the judge of the micro.

Anybody, who has been to a house of mirrors at any visiting carnival, can understand the inaccuracy of projections, but Freeman goes one step further and questions the blueprint of the mirror designer. Hence, informing that the mirrors are simply illusions shaped by a blind mirror-maker.

Other writings explore the difference between defining self as victim versus survivor. "My Purpose – My Pain," does not allow the offended to become solely defined by the offense. Her concept of purpose takes on a deeper meaning when she proposes how a victim can be transformed into a sublime survivor, thus robbing the offender of their role of giving pain and, worse yet, demanding that the victim keep carrying that pain. She articulates how survivors become liberators leading others out of hell.

In order to avoid the trap of hypocrisy inherent in the matrix, the piece titled, "The 'I do that too!' Principle" places Freeman in a courageous role where she states her own flaws, thus making her seem more authentic and real. Something the matrix does not want- real. In Freeman's world, the expert and the authority reside within the spirit of the person. Like her namesake, Freeman, the author is defining a path where we can all be free from man-made matrixes and embrace a divinely created reality.

Having worked in a spectrum of fields, serving an array of people with diverse experiences on both the national and international stage, I am in the rightful position to strongly state that the principles within this book can speak to a refugee in Sudan as easily as it can speak to a drug addict in America. Rejection, hopelessness, and fear are globally experienced, but hope, redemption and love are universally felt. Despite the stubborn stronghold of the matrix, it is not invincible. It has tremendous weaknesses, which are already being exposed with the weapon of illuminating awareness, manifested through people like Anneshia Freeman. This book will serve as an inoculation against the matrix. Opening this book will open your world up to so much more than is currently seen.

Carol Chehade, LCSW
Licensed Clinical Social Worker
Writer and Film/Theater Producer
Miami, Florida

Carol Chehade is the creator of the nationally acclaimed theatrical production entitled "My Real Name."

Introduction

My name is Anneshia Freeman. I am the author of this book, and I am a survivor. I have survived a childhood of mental, emotional, sexual, physical, and spiritual abuse. I have survived years of drug and alcohol addiction. I have been clean for 12 years (written in 2012), and I have successfully resocialized myself into what sociologists refer to as "the dominant culture."

Since walking away from the streets in August of 2000, I have completed an associate's degree in computer application technology, a bachelor's degree in business, a master's degree in business administration, and a master's degree in social work – all of which were completed summa cum laude. I am also a certified alcohol and drug counselor. I WAS the addict that the other addicts talked about – the dope-man took me to treatment. My life stands as a testament that there is no "us and them," there is "we" – we the people.

This book contains a collection of 31 articles that I wrote for my column in the Grand Rapids Times newspaper. My column is entitled *What's Really Going On*, which also happens to be the name of this book. What's Really Going On (WRGO) is a slang term I learned during my 15-year participant/observation, exploratory, ethnographic research study of several inner-city Detroit subcultures. WRGO means the follows:

> There is something going on that's not right. I am not sure what it is because it is carefully disguised as something good, but my gut instinct is saying, "Something is not right." Therefore, I am making a declaration in the form of a question to let you know that I know something is terribly wrong. I have not figured it out all the way, but I am sorting through the overlay and I promise you, I am going to find out what's really going on!

The first eight articles in the book are from *The Matrix* series, which is a collection of articles and sermons I have written based on the movie by the same name. I watched the movie *The Matrix* years ago when a man picked me up off the streets of Detroit and paid me to go to his apartment in the suburbs and watch this movie. This man paid me several hundred dollars to do nothing but watch *The Matrix*. Then he sent me back to the "hood" in a cab with a VHS copy of the movie and enough money to appease the street creditors who would want a payment for my lack of work during the night. I knew the movie contained "keys" and I stored them in my brain, knowing that one-day the locks would be revealed.

The other 23 articles contained in this book are all written in the vein of cognitive restructuring and resocialization. Some of the articles were written for a secular audience while some were written from a spiritual perspective. All of the articles are meant to enlighten, challenge, and inspire. Please come with me on a journey into the light to see "What's Really Going On!"

What Do You Define As Real?
Part I – in the Matrix Series

"Reality, leaves a lot to the imagination"

- John Lennon

It has been my personal experience that my reality was often an illusion produced by my distorted thought process. In the movie the Matrix, Morpheus took Neo inside the Matrix and Neo asked Morpheus "Is this real?" Morpheus responded to Neo's question with a question of his own, "How do you define real? If you're talking about what you can feel, what you can smell, what you can taste and see, then real is simply electrical signals interpreted by your brain." What was Morpheus trying to help Neo understand? He was telling Neo, "Whatever your mind codes and categorizes as real is what is real to you."

In my past, I often coded and categorized maltreatment that I received from others as evidence of my defectiveness as a person – that was my realty based on my distorted thought process. My reality was, "I am being rejected by others because of personal flaws." Since I have made significant progress in restructuring my thought process, I now categorize and code those past experiences with manipulative, self-seeking people differently. My reality now is, "In the past I suffered from low-self esteem. I gave off unconscious clues to others as to how I felt about myself. Manipulative, self-seeking people picked up on those clues and profited off my unaddressed issues. There was something wrong with my self-concept – not with me. In addition, I can take the halo off because, just like I learned the victim role in my childhood, I also learned the villain role. Both roles were enacted in my home daily. I have been the manipulative self-seeking person on another set. That hurtful relationship in which I was mistreated was just a reproduction of a script from my childhood – *Wounded Little Girl Gets Hurt Again*." THIS IS MY REALTY now about my past experiences – get it?

Let me share another example. In the past, when I was defining my reality out of my distorted thought process, I would be in the fetal position, in torment because a particular man left me for another woman. My reality was something like this, "He left me for someone else. There is something wrong with me. There is something right with her. They will be happy together. She has what I lack. They are probably riding off into the sunset right now on a white horse with Michael McDonald singing in the background – I want to know what love is….." For me, at that point in time, my reality was, "I have been rejected. She has been accepted." My reality about that past is much different today. Based on what I define as real today, my reality about those past relationships is as follows, "He was only with me in the first place for what he could get out of me. He was probably taught the P.I.M.P (Power In Manipulating People) game in his childhood, and he has been conditioned to believe that he cannot support himself sufficiently in any other manner. The person he left me for, more than likely, has the same issues I have or she would not have attracted the same caliber of man I did. All three of us needed some help."

Let me share a couple more examples. Many people's realty is that exercise is too hard. They define exercise as too hard – so their reality of obesity is created by what they define as "too hard." What if they began defining being obese and having multiple health problems as "too hard?" Then their reality would be that exercising one hour a day five to six times a week is less painful than being miserable all day every day. Many people define college as "too hard," so their reality is that they live in poverty their entire lives because of what they code and categorize as "too hard." What if they sent their brain a different signal? What if they defined poverty as TOO HARD, not having a sense of purpose as TOO HARD, being unfulfilled as TOO HARD. What if they signaled their brain that college is CHALLENGING but DOABLE? What if they defined four years of pain as NOTHING compared to 60 or 70 years of MISERY – struggling in poverty? Allow me the pleasure of answering those last few questions. Their realty would be, "School is challenging, hard, but doable. What is too hard is being at the mercy of someone else's decision the rest of my life." As one of my mentors says quite often, "It's hard to see the picture when you're the frame." Your thought process is framing your reality.

The Blind Mind Syndrome
Part II – in the Matrix Series

"My darkness has been filled with the light of intelligence, and behold, the outer day-lit world was stumbling and groping in social blindness."

- Helen Keller

This is part II in the Matrix Series. For those not familiar with the movie or for those who thought it was a karate flick, Morpheus defined the Matrix as, "…the world that has been pulled over your eyes to blind you from the truth." In the movie, after Neo had been "unplugged" from the "world system" he asked Morpheus a question, "Why do my eyes hurt?" Morpheus answered Neo, "You've never used them before." What did Morpheus mean by that? Neo was not a physically blind man when he was "plugged" into the Matrix. Morpheus was explaining to Neo that he had been "plugged" into a system that blinded his mind. Only people who have been "unplugged" can see "what's really going on." There is a verse in the Bible that talks about this phenomenon, II Corinthians 4:4 AMP – "For the god of this world has blinded the unbeliever's minds [that they should not discern the truth]..."aka – THE BLIND MIND SYNDROME!

As a child, I was raised in a very dysfunctional household where I was physically, mentally, emotional, sexually, and spiritually abused. I was also raised in the church, and one of my abusers was a religious fanatic that made me read the Bible for hours daily. My family was poor, but I was raised around wealthy, Caucasian people. This dichotomy of experience caused me to have partial sight as the man in the Bible who said he saw "men as trees walking." My mother (the religious fanatic) found the keys (the truth), but she did not know how to use them. She gave me the keys, but she did NOT demonstrate how to use them, and because she was completely "locked up," I thought the keys were useless. When I went to the streets and got caught up with drugs, I saw things that other people did not see. There was so much light deposited in me that I could still partially see even though I was bound. I thought everyone could see what I saw. I was WRONG! I was frequently reprimanded for sharing my observations with the blind (story of my life). Now that I can see clearly, sometimes my eyes hurt – Plato's Allegory of the Cave – but my eyes are adjusting.

Let me give you an example. Many young blind minds believe they can sell drugs or commit other crimes and be the ONE who "gets away." They appear to not be able to SEE people all around them being shot, going to prison, becoming RIP t-shirts, etc. They "jump off the cliff" right behind the others who have jumped to their demise. They race to their destruction with their "eyes wide shut." They walk right past the university where they could spend two, four, six, eight years mastering a skill that would enable them to have a good life and go sit in a prison cell for 20 years. Why, you ask? How can they not SEE...THE BLIND MIND SYNDROME! People who can SEE have an OBLIGATION to help them SEE! They haven't been "unplugged," so they cannot see or hear. If I listen to a rap song encouraging me to sell drugs, trying to convince me that I will be a "big baller, shot caller," I know that is a lie. I know the penitentiary and the graveyard is the harvest for that lifestyle. We who can SEE because of the "illuminating truth of the gospel" have a responsibility to develop creative ways to help the blind SEE.

One of the things I do to assist the young, often court mandated, youth in my cognitive restructuring and resocialization program is design skits to help them SEE the self-destructive cycles they are living. I take them to the Chicago Mercantile Exchange so they can SEE people "flipping" wheat, corn, soybean, pigs, and cows. They can SEE they do not have to "flip" poison to their people to make money. I take them to the Federal Reserve to SEE money being printed and shredded, so they can SEE they are killing each other for a piece of paper that is printed and destroyed daily. I take them to Michigan State University so they can SEE other youth who grew up in crack-houses with drug-addicted parents at college "walking it down!" If you can see, and you walk past a blind person who is about to step in an uncovered manhole, would you keep walking...shaking your head about their impending doom; or would you try to help them SEE?

Proverbs 24:11-12 Amplified Bible (AMP)
11 Deliver those who are drawn away to death, and

those who totter to the slaughter, hold them back [from their doom].

12 If you [profess ignorance and] say, Behold, we did not know this, does not He Who weighs and ponders the heart perceive and consider it? And He Who guards your life, does not He know it? And shall not He render to [you and] every man according to his works?

This is a Training Simulation
Part III – in the Matrix Series

"Learning is experience.
Everything else is just information."

- Albert Einstein

This is part III in the Matrix Series. In the movie, The Matrix, Neo was being trained in order to assist the team in fighting the Matrix – the system that was enslaving people. After an extensive session of having information downloaded into his brain, he told Morpheus, his mentor, "I know Kung-fu!" Morpheus responded to Neo's declaration by saying, "Show me!" He then proceeded to take Neo into a computer program simulation that would enable him to demonstrate what he claimed he had learned. Morpheus said to Neo, "This is a sparring program, similar to the programmed reality of the Matrix." At another point in the movie, Morpheus referred to this program as "a training simulation." Neo had some information and thought he was ready for battle. Morpheus, who knew Neo had extraordinary capabilities, also knew that he needed to have an opportunity to practice what he had learned – to operationalize the information he had received. Morpheus knew, as any good mentor does, that knowing and doing are two completely different things. Let's go deeper...

One of the classes I took for my degree in Computer Application's Technology was entitled Systems Analysis. My instructor started the class by announcing that he did not give tests. Half of the class looked pleased while the other half of the class displayed looks of disbelief. My instructor completed his statement by saying, "But I will give you five opportunities to display personal knowledge." What he was saying was, "I am going to teach you some strategies to use in order to analyze a system. You, as a student wishing to pass this class, will claim that you understand this information and that you are ready to move forward to the next level in the program. In order for me to allow you to pass to the next level, I am going to design a situation in which you will be forced to display the knowledge you say you have." In other words, my instructor was providing me with a training simulation – a sparring program. He was giving me an opportunity to operationalize, in a controlled environment, the information I had received before I was put into the real situation for which I was being trained.

In life, we receive information from various sources. We go to school, church, conferences, and workshops. We listen to CDs, read the Bible, read spiritual books, read secular books, and the list goes on. We have plenty of information, but do we recognize the opportunities we are given to operationalize the information we have downloaded into our brains? Do not make the mistake of thinking that you are ready for battle because you KNOW something. You need numerous opportunities to practice what you know so that you can internalize the information.

For example, I received information by reading a book by a noted neurologist and psychologist about the brain. This doctor said that our brain contains a record of all of the facial expressions, vocal tones, and voice inflections we encountered repeatedly during our childhood. That record also contains the emotional responses associated with those stimuli. After reading that part of the book, I said to myself, "I now know why I feel angry, hurt, intimidated, and/or threatened by certain facial expressions, vocal tones, and voice inflections. I can now respond properly as opposed to reacting inappropriately." Well guess what, I am given training simulations daily – opportunities to "display personal knowledge." Meaning: when someone I do not know gives me a dirty look, it is a training simulation, an opportunity to display personal knowledge. I am powerless over what people choose to do with their facial expressions. Do I intend to ask everyone who gives me a dirty look what that look means? Do I really have that kind of time? Or, will I realize that the mean look activated the part of my brain that contains all the mean looks my mother gave me and all the mean looks the popular kids at grade school gave me? Will I remember the information I learned from the doctor when a fellow student in the hallway at the university gives me a dirty look and activates the emotional responses that I felt as a child? Will I tell myself, "This is a training simulation – a sparring program – keep walking down the hall to your class – DISPLAY PERSONAL KNOWLEDGE?" Or, am I going to allow the stimulus to activate me to the point where campus security is called, and I'm on the cover of the "Busted" magazine?

In life, you are given training simulations daily – opportunities to display personal knowledge. For example, you say you know that you are supposed to love the unlovable. Well guess what...you will be given a training simulation – an opportunity to display personal knowledge. You say you know "No weapon formed against you will prosper," well guess what...the weapon will be formed – a training simulation – an opportunity to display personal knowledge. You say you know that, "Greater is He that is within you than he who is in the world," well guess what – he who is in the world, Goliath, is going to come against you – this is a training simulation – an opportunity to display personal knowledge. Challenges you encounter are simply saying, "You say you have some information in this area – SHOW ME!" Or challenges in life are simply saying, "You need some information in this area...get some and then practice using it." As Johann Wolfgang von Goethe says, "Knowing is not enough; we must apply. Willing is not enough; we must do."

Who Are the Agents?
Anyone Who Hasn't Been Unplugged
Part IV – in the Matrix Series

"The greatest revolution of our generation is the discovery that human beings, by changing the inner attitudes of their minds, can change the outer aspects of their lives.

- William James

This week's column is Part IV in the Matrix Series. In the movie the Matrix, Morpheus was preparing Neo to fight the system with another training simulation. In this particular simulation, Neo was learning about the people inside the Matrix. Morpheus was walking through crowds of people with Neo following closely behind, looking at the people while Morpheus talked. As they were walking, Morpheus was explaining to Neo that the individuals around them were part of the Matrix; and although they were trying to free the minds of those people, many of them were not ready to be "unplugged." As Morpheus was talking, Neo lost focus because he was looking at a beautiful woman in a red dress. Morpheus asked Neo if he was listening to him or looking at the woman in the red dress. As Neo begin fumbling for words, Morpheus told Neo, "Look again." When Neo looked again, the woman in the red dress was an agent with a gun pointed at Neo's head. Morpheus explained to Neo, "Anyone we haven't unplugged is a potential agent."

How can we apply this scene and this powerful quote to our lives today? Well, I'm glad you asked. Morpheus was teaching Neo to stay focused on their mission and to understand that anyone who is not privy to the truth, is "plugged" into the system and that makes them an enemy. Some people are plugged into a system that believes that a number of people have to suffer for others to live well. I have met these people. They have tried to explain their reasoning to me, attempting to convince me to "get me on board" with the program. They have not been "unplugged" in their thinking as it relates to the term "currency." They are thinking that, in order to have wealth on their level, they must keep certain people on another level. They are not thinking of the term "currency" as "transmission from person to person as a medium of exchange – circulation." The term currency means flow. People who do not believe in others advancing have not been "unplugged" in their thinking as it relates to the FLOW. It is ego at its worst for any person or group of people to believe that just because they do not know how to do something, it cannot be done. Meaning: just because they do not know how to design a system, allowing for the steady advancement of people from level to level, does not mean that system cannot be designed. Let's discuss a few more examples.

There are some people, "potential agents," who have not been "unplugged" in their thinking as it relates to their worth and value as a person. Say for example a woman is "plugged" into a system that tricked her into thinking her worth and value are connected to her sexuality. If another attractive woman walks into the room, the woman who has not been "unplugged," as to her true worth and value as a person, will most likely feel anger, resentment, and jealousy simply because another attractive woman walked into the room. The system told her that the attractive woman who walked into the room just took some of her value. The woman who has not been "unplugged" is a "potential agent" who may try to cause harm to a woman she does not know who has done nothing to her – simply because of her beauty. If the same woman becomes "unplugged" in her thinking and realizes that her sexuality is just one aspect of who she is and that her worth and value lie in her unique assignment on this earth, she is no longer a "potential agent" to other attractive women.

If a person is "plugged" into thinking that their worth and value are dependent upon their latest and greatest accomplishment and they hear about someone else's great accomplishment, that person may experience envy, anger, resentment, and fear. That person may try to cause harm to the person their thinking has told them is a threat. The harm can be a cynical look, character assassination, or a discouraging word. If a person becomes "unplugged" in this area and realizes that their sense of worth and value is dependent on how they view themselves and not on what they DO, they can enjoy the accomplishments of others. They are no longer an "agent" on a mission to harm people who are doing great things.

Another example of people who have not been "unplugged" is individuals who believe that certain ethnic groups are not as capable as other ethnic groups. These people have not been "unplugged" in their thinking as it relates to an ingrained sense of superiority. They are very dangerous to people they claim they want to help. They may actually believe they are helping people by constantly giving them a "fish" because they do not believe those individuals have the capacity to "learn how to fish." The "plugged-in agents," who are depriving others of developing self-sufficiency, are sincere in their desire to "help" but they are sincerely wrong in their approach. If those people were "unplugged," then their "helping" methodologies would change. They would develop "helping" programs based on the same principles they use in their lives to be successful – such as discipline, structure, sacrifice, endurance, persistence, etc.

There are many people (agents) in the church who have not been "unplugged" as it relates to "for all have sinned and come short..." so they turn their noses up at certain people God is delivering and bringing into His house. They "shoot" people with their facial expressions, vocal tone, and voice inflection. There are some people in the church who have not been "unplugged" as it relates to food so they fix "heart-attack, high blood pressure, cancer" dinners after a healing service – they are DANGEROUS. So what is the solution – AND YE SHALL KNOW THE TRUTH, AND THE TRUTH SHALL SET YOU FREE! As Oliver Wendell Holmes Jr. puts it, “Man's mind, once stretched by a new idea, never regains its original dimensions.”

Residual Self-Image - RSI
Part V – in the Matrix Series

"Self-image sets the boundaries of individual accomplishment."

- Maxwell Maltz

This week's column is Part V in the Matrix Series. For those unfamiliar with the movie or for those who thought it was an action thriller, Morpheus defined the Matrix as, "...the world that has been pulled over your eyes to blind you from the truth." There was a scene in the movie when Morpheus took Neo into the "construct," their loading program, to show him some things. Neo looked around in amazement and said, "Right now we are in a computer?" Morpheus told Neo that his hair and clothes were different, that what he was seeing was his "residual self-image...the mental projection of his digital self." Morpheus was telling Neo that, while they were in the Matrix, the image of himself that he was seeing was the image that the "system" had programmed him to see. Neo looked totally different when he was not inside the Matrix, when he was "unplugged." Another source that I found defined "Residual Self-image (RSI)" as, "The subjective appearance of a human while connected to the Matrix."

For the purpose of this week's column, we will discuss RSI in terms of how people are often programmed to think of themselves, "When they were a child." When I was a child, I was programmed to think the following things about myself (to name a few):

- There is something wrong with me.
- There is something wrong with everything I do. Nothing will turn out right.
- Compared to others, I come up short.
- I am not entitled to the same rights, opportunities, and privileges as others.
- I deserve second best.
- My value as a person is connected to my sexuality (and so forth).

This "digital coding" was programmed into my "self-image" aka "my unconscious self-concept." I have approximately 150 negative, self-image codes that were a part of my "Residual Self-Image." This programming kept me living a dysfunctional life for years. I was endowed, before the foundation of the world, with various gifts and talents "wheat" that was choked by my RSI "tares." The wheat and the tares grew together. The Matrix could not take my gifts so it had to sow syntax errors into my self-image coding in order to keep me from operating at maximum efficiency. What a waste to society!

Today I have reprogrammed my RSI. "How did I do that," you ask? Well, I am glad you asked! It was with the truth. You see, the old RSI was comprised of lies. John 8: 32 And ye shall <u>KNOW</u> the truth, and the truth shall set you free. If <u>knowing</u> the truth will set you free, it MUST be a lie that has you bound. For 36 years, my life was a "mental projection of my digital self." As a man thinketh, so is he. I lived the life my RSI told me I was capable of living. I was a societal liability instead of the asset I could have been. Is that why we are in debt as a country? Could it be an RSI problem? We have genius' standing on the corner due to syntax errors!

The truths that counteract the lies that comprised my RSI are as follows:

- There is something wrong with everybody.
    - For all have sinned...

- I have ample proof I can do many things correctly. I got high "correctly" for 15 years. If I can execute a dysfunctional plan and bring it to pass, I can do the same thing with a life-enhancing plan. The same principles are at work.
    - I can do all things through Christ...
- Compared to others, I come up me. My value is in my individuality – the uniqueness God designed.
    - Before I formed you in your mother's womb, I knew you...
- I am entitled to whatever rights, opportunities, and privileges my Daddy (aka God) says I can have.
    - The earth is the Lord's and the fullness thereof...
- I deserve what God says I deserve.
    - I would above all that you prosper and be in health!
- My value is based on the criteria I choose to believe.
    - You are a chosen generation, a royal priesthood...

Do not allow an RSI riddled with syntax errors to determine the quality of your life. Refuse to live a "rellusion" (a realty that is actually an illusion based on a distorted thought process). Syntax errors can be fixed. When I did my computer-programming final in 2002, the program would not work for two weeks because I was using the wrong code. The program would highlight the incorrect code in RED LETTERS and say, "You have a syntax error." I did not realize at the time that God was sending me a message about my life. The new code you need is in the Word, it is on billboards, it is on television commercials, it is in secular and Christian books – the truth is all around you. You have to renew your mind to reprogram your RSI, and that requires work. Maxwell Maltz says, "The "self-image" is the key to human personality and human behavior. Change the self-image and you change the personality and the behavior." Denis Waitley gives us the formula, "Relentless, repetitive self talk is what changes our self-image." The formula works whether we are saying the truth or repeating the syntax errors. You have the power to CHOOSE what you say to yourself!

Focus is a Weapon!
Part VI - Matrix Series

"I don't care how much power, brilliance or energy you have, if you don't harness it and focus it on a specific target, and hold it there you're never going to accomplish as much as your ability warrants."

- Zig Zilgar

This week's article is part VI in the Matrix Series. The Matrix is defined as, "The world that has been pulled over your eyes to blind you from the truth." In the opening scene of the movie, Trinity, a person who has been "unplugged" from the world system, is in a room. She has been setup by someone who was supposedly on the team. She was on the phone with her leader Morpheus telling him that she had been set up. He informed her that he was aware of her situation but told her that she needed to get to another exit. Trinity asked Morpheus if there were agents. Morpheus said, "Yes. You have to focus." He then told her where the next exit was and assured her that she could make it. If you read my other articles in the Matrix series, you are familiar with the "agents." The agents are the forces of darkness that children of light are sent to conquer in whatever sphere of influence they are assigned. Any person, who has not been "unplugged," is a potential agent (vessel) that the forces of darkness can use to come against a son or daughter of Zion. I found it very interesting and quite profound that Morpheus told Trinity to FOCUS in order to get away from the agents and get to her next destination. He did not tell her to use a certain karate move (she had already been trained in karate moves) – he told her to FOCUS.

One of the greatest tools of the enemy to keep you from fulfilling your purpose is distractions – it is the "hocus pocus – distract and defocus" trick. Some people are distracted by negative people or things that gets them off course for years. Then they spend more years dealing with the consequences of their decisions. They fell for the "hocus pocus – distract and defocus." Other people become distracted and defocused doing positive things that have absolutely nothing to do with their Kingdom Assignment. They are doing "good" things, but not God ordered things. For example, a person may be assigned to wage war for the Kingdom of God in the medical industry as a doctor. That means that person must go to school and FOCUS on school for a long time. It could be very easy for that person to become distracted being on 17 committees in the church when that person is supposed to be on duty preparing for their assignment in this earth realm. There is nothing wrong with being on committees at church; but during the season that person is called to be at medical school, if they are super busy on committees, they are falling for the "hocus pocus distract and defocus" trick. While they are on all these different committees, working at a low-paying, dead-end job that was only meant to sustain them while they prepared for their assignment in the medical industry, the other team has their people FOCUSING at medical school. That's right – Dr. Darkness is walking across the stage with his medical degree reporting for duty. Now, that's too bad!

Let me give you another example. I was watching a detective show on television one night (the one night a week I allowed myself to breath when I was in school). They were doing an episode about a pedophile ring. One of the villains in this episode went to law school, AND GRADUATED, so he could find loopholes in the law to help his fellow predators avoid prison. Can you imagine the type of focus it took for this agent of darkness to complete law school? While watching this show, I imagined this to be a real life situation and wondered if there was a child of God on duty at law school preparing to fight darkness in the legal field. The enemy will not always be as obvious as getting a son or daughter of Zion hooked on drugs and alcohol (although that's a trick he uses often). Sometimes the enemy will defocus a person with commendable endeavors – as long as he can keep that person from being on assignment in their field. You know, the field where their gift will make room for them.

Pastor Joel Brooks Jr. uses the analogy of church being akin to being in a huddle on a football field. After we break from the huddle – we are suppose to battle the other team – not sit down on the sideline having tea and crumpets planning the next huddle while the other team wins the game. Your "game," your "field" is whatever sphere of influence you are assigned to affect – have dominion and be fruitful. Go ye into the world – that requires focus, training, preparation, and discipline. The enemy cannot take your gift because that is something God gave you. Therefore, the enemy has to use tricks. He has many tricks, but distractions is a "play" he runs over and over and over again. It takes focus to prepare for your assignment. It takes focus to operate in your assignment.

Let me clarify something. I attend church, I attend conferences when I can (or I catch it streaming live), I read all sorts of books, and I have an awesome CD and DVD collection; but, when I needed to be at the University preparing for my Kingdom Assignment, I was in class. When I was not in class, I was studying, writing papers, and so forth. Guess what I was doing. I was worshiping. The law of first mention – worship is sacrifice. We need to go to central headquarters (church, conferences) and get the orders (spiritual instructions) from the generals (our spiritual leaders), and we need to have our own person huddles (time along with God). If you were in a restaurant and the waitress was going from table to table taking orders but never went to the kitchen and filled the orders, you would feel like you were in the Twilight Zone – right! Too many people have notebooks full of sermon notes, scripture references, faith declarations, and positive affirmations, but they are not filling the orders!

Do not allow distractions to keep you from doing what you know you are supposed to be doing to fulfill your destiny. That is a trick of the enemy. Focus is a weapon. I am done with school for a while so now I am FOCUSING on the next thing I have been commanded to do. Do not allow others who are not on duty to get you off duty. They will try to get you off duty so they will not feel bad or look bad. You will have to tell some people, "I am not available! I'm about my Father's business!" Let's end with a quote by Bruce Lee, "The successful warrior is the average man, with laser-like focus."

Stop Trying To Hit It...and Hit It!
Part VII – Matrix Series

"Try not. Do, or do not. There is no try."

- Yoda

In the sparring program scene in the Matrix, Morpheus was testing Neo's skill set in Kung-fu. When the scene began, Morpheus explained the program to Neo, and then said, "Hit me if you can." What Morpheus was saying to Neo was, "I'm your target; now hit the target – if you can." During the fight, Morpheus offered input such as "Good! Adaptation, improvisation – your weakness is not your technique." At one point when Morpheus took a break from whipping on Neo, He asked Neo a question, "How did I beat you?" Neo said, "You're too fast." Morpheus replied to Neo with a question, "Do you believe that my being stronger or faster has anything to do with my muscles in this place?" The "place" was the Matrix – a program in the mind. As the fight progressed, Morpheus said, "What are you waiting for, you are faster than this – don't think you are, know you are." After a few more punches, Morpheus said, frustrated, "Come on! Stop trying to hit me and hit me!" Now, let's apply this to real life situations.

What Morpheus was saying to Neo is that he had two very important ingredients in his technique – adaptation and improvisation. He implied that Neo had a weakness but it was not his technique. Later, Morpheus identified Neo's weakness – his thought process. Neo was TRYING to do something he could DO, but he did not fully believe in himself. Morpheus informed Neo that being faster or stronger has nothing to do with MINDSET MUSCLE. I have known some "straight-up gangsters" who could not deal with a dirty look in an environment where physical altercations are unacceptable and foul you out of the game. Meaning: I know some people who were dangerous in the streets, but cannot deal with someone giving them a condescending look when they walk into a room at the university or at the office. Get the point – MINDSET MUSCLE. The "recovering gangster" may be faster and stronger and have flawless technique, but if their mind is weak, if they do not believe in themselves – they can be beat! Eleanor Roosevelt, who had MINDSET MUSCLE, would have processed the condescending look by saying to herself, "No one can make you feel inferior without your consent" and kept it moving.

Now let us address the "TRYING" part of the equation. In the fight simulation, Morpheus was playing the target, which Neo would face in the Matrix – the agents. So, the goal was for Neo to hit the target. Neo did okay periodically, but in the long haul Morpheus would get the best of him. Why was Neo unsuccessful at hitting the target? Neo was unsuccessful because he was TRYING to do something instead of DOING something. How many times do people say they are TRYING to do something they have the capability to DO? As I was thinking about writing this article, I thought back to the 15 years I smoked crack, and I can NEVER think of a time when I said I was going to TRY to get high. In fact, I do not remember discussing my plans for drug usage, because it was a given. If I did for some reason mention my plans, it was "I'm GOING to get high!" It was – no doubt – it's going down! That was my attitude. It did not matter if I had zero dollars, "rookie officer morality" patrolling the streets, serial killer stalking, dope boys looking for me who I owed money – IT'S GOING DOWN – NO MATTER

WHAT! Now think if we had that attitude about our laudable goals! That was the piece Morpheus told Neo he was missing, "Don't think you are...**<u>KNOW</u>** you are!"

How many of us are TRYING to lose weight? How many of us KNOW how to lose weight? I am going to give you and me the secret to weight loss. You eat less and burn more! BAM – and you thought it was more complicated than that – right. Okay, what else are we trying to do? How many people are trying to stop smoking cigarettes? I am not being judgmental. I smoked cigarettes for years. I know it's hard – hard is not synonymous with impossible. I stopped ten years ago. I stopped trying to quit, and I quit. I weaned myself off, but I did not TRY to wean myself off – I WEANED MYSELF OFF with the help of God! Find the method that works for you, and stop TRYING to stop smoking and STOP smoking.

Now, let us identify a few more targets we tend to miss because we are TRYING to do what we are capable of DOING. How many people are trying to leave negative people alone? I do not have negative people in my life, because I stop TRYING to leave negatrons alone. I

STOPPED associating with them! It took a while for me to get good and tired of TRYING to leave manipulators alone, but I finally had it and ended years of abuse with a 60-second phone call. Okay...when you stop laughing at me, we can continue. I know people who are small in physical stature and are very soft-spoken, but have tremendous MENTAL MUSCLE and will very nicely, in a soft tone, tell a manipulator, "No!" End of conversation! Wow, how many of us are in situations that are destroying our schedule and budget that could be shut down in two seconds with a two-letter word, "No." Stop TRYING to say no and SAY, "No!" Okay, let's pull it all together.

Morpheus told Neo that he was strong, fast, and had flawless technique. He also told Neo that his weakness was that he was TRYING to do something he was capable of DOING – if he believed in himself. Hey, let's stop TRYING to do things we have the capability to DO and just DO it. Don't think you can, KNOW you can! Edmund Hillary put it this way, "It is not the mountain we conquer but ourselves."

Downloading – Accessing the Mainframe
Part VIII – Matrix Series

"When all think alike, then no one is thinking."

- Walter Lippman

In the movie "The Matrix," there is a scene when Trinity and Neo are attempting to rescue Morpheus from the agents who are holding him captive. In order to execute their plan, they needed to use a helicopter that was parked nearby. Neo asked Trinity, "Do you know how to fly that thing?" Trinity responded, "Not yet." She then proceeded to call their headquarters and say, "I need a pilot program for a B-2(12) helicopter – HURRY!" She closed her eyes, and the operator, Tank, who was stationed at headquarters, downloaded the instructions to Trinity. While Tank was downloading the instructions, the camera alternated between Trinity's body that was sitting in the chair at headquarters and her body that was inside the Matrix receiving the download. You see, Trinity was two places at the same time. She was seated in a chair at headquarters and plugged into the Matrix simultaneously – in the world but not of the world. Trinity opened her eyes after the download was complete and said, "Let's go!" She had the information necessary to operate the helicopter.

I know that as a Daughter of Zion, according to Matthew 16:19, I have access to the "Keys of the Kingdom." If I have these keys, I can use them to bind and loose in the earth realm. The Amplified Bible says it like this, "I will give you the keys of the kingdom of heaven; and whatever you bind (declare to be improper and unlawful) on earth must be what is already bound in heaven; and whatever you loose (declare lawful) on earth must be what is already loosed in heaven." Do you see the connection to the scene in "The Matrix?" Not yet...okay, let's go deeper.

There are some diseases that need to be bound on earth – cancer, diabetes, high blood pressure – that's the medical field. There are some things that need to be bound in the education field. If you work in the foster care field, the criminal justice field, the food field, and so forth, you know there are some things in those industries that need to be bound. James 1:5 says that if we lack wisdom, all we have to do is ask God for that wisdom – aka – the download. If you are assigned to a certain sphere of influences – you are specially designed and equipped to affect change in that industry. The problem is that too many people conform to the norm – the world's (The Matrix) standard. Romans 12:2 in the Amplified Bible says, "Do not be conformed to this world (this age), [fashioned after and adapted to its external, superficial customs], but be transformed (changed) by the [entire] renewal of your mind [by its new ideals and its new attitude], so that you may prove [for yourselves] what is the good and acceptable and perfect will of God, even the thing which is good and acceptable and perfect [in His sight for you]."

I am assigned to affect change in the human service industry on the micro, mezzo, and macro levels. The methodologies and ideologies that I use were downloaded from the throne room. God downloads so fast that at times I become overwhelmed and have to ask Him to help me slow down and put things in perspective. Sister Thedia Fields told me some years ago to put five blank notebooks by my bed because God was going to download some information to me. Ladies and Gentlemen – those notebooks are filled. Some of the downloads are already in operation as programs, trainings, workbooks, belief system cards, and so forth. I cannot take credit for this information. I am the trustee for these Kingdom concepts "keys" in this earth realm, and I take my job as trustee seriously – ask my copyright, trademark lawyer. I was "locked-up" when God gave me the "keys." Look at God! I got delivered proofreading the first 400-page manual the Holy Spirit wrote through me. PLEASE HEAR ME! I saw, really saw, some of the information for the first time when I proofread it. Come on now – I had only been off drugs for two years when God downloaded those concepts through me! I got my credentials in that industry after I developed the program☺. It does not have to happen in that order, but I know for certainty that God wanted to get all the glory for the *Lies That Bind*® Program. So, He created it first so no educational institution could take credit.

Thy KINGDOM come – Thy will be done on earth as it is in heaven. According to Ephesians 2:6, we are seated in heavenly places by virtue of being in Christ Jesus, just as Trinity was seated in the Nebuchadnezzar (the name of their ship/headquarters) while she was in

"The Matrix" acting on the downloads. That means we have access to the Kingdom storeroom that has the "keys" for whatever industry we are assigned to impact on the earth. The church is **ONE** sphere of influence – it is headquarters. Some people are assigned to run and operate headquarters. That is where the rest of us, who are assigned to other spheres of influence, go to get the access codes to the mainframe to get the downloads for our sphere of influence. The rest of us, not assigned to headquarters as our vocation, are to be about our Father's business in the medical field, the food and nutrition field, the social work field, the criminal justice field, the physical fitness field, the youth services field, and so forth. Our field is also where our money is. Bishop Jakes says, "Bring God what He ordered, and he will pay for it and give you a tip!" Pastor Joel Brooks Junior preaches – Work Your Field!

Harvey Firestone put it like this, "Capital isn't so important in business. Experience isn't so important. You can get both these things. What is important is ideas. If you have ideas, you have the main asset you need, and there isn't any limit to what you can do with your business and your life." You, as a Son or Daughter of Zion, have access to Kingdom concepts – ideologies and methodologies. Call headquarters, and ask the operator to download what you need. Then go ye into the world and preach the gospel! What is the gospel – The Kingdom of God is at hand!

Unlearning What is Untrue And Ye Shall Know the Truth

"The most useful piece of learning for the uses of life is to unlearn what is untrue."

- Antisthenes

Many individuals are trapped in self-defeating patterns, such as drug addiction, drug dealing, and negative relationships with no understanding of why they keep doing the same things over and over and over again, despite the consequences. If the truth will set you free (John 8:32), it MUST be a lie that has you bound (implied theology). Wanting to free themselves, seeking to change, some of the afflicted load up on self-help books, self-help CDs and DVDs, attend seminars and conferences, but to no avail – the self-destruction continues. What's really going on? Maybe Antisthenes was on to something. Maybe before a mind can make room to store, activate, and apply new information, the old useless data that is clogging the hard drive needs to be exposed and extracted. Perhaps the secret for some individuals lies in a sequence of actions. The first thing many individuals who are suffering from self-defeating, self-sabotaging behaviors need to do, before shoveling in new information, is expose the "untrue" and "unlearn" the lie.

Dr. R. Joseph, noted expert in the field of neuroscience and psychology, argues that adults make decisions, whether positive or negative, based on unconscious programming they received during the formative years. The information, whether positive or negative, that is stored in the right brain as a belief system, comes from what they observed others around them doing and how they were treated. In adulthood, that information is constantly accessed and makes decisions for the person without their conscious awareness (Joseph, 1992). Another noted Christian psychologist, Dr. Ed Smith (2000), refers to the negative, unconscious beliefs as lies,

> "Where do the lies come from? How do they originate? How did they find their way into the early childhood events of a person's life? It often comes from the child's own thinking and personal interpretation of what happened. Children will almost always misinterpret life. This

> misinterpretation is not the fault of the child since he or she is incapable of making true interpretations about life. As a parent, I am responsible to see that my children interpret life correctly. I must pass on to my child daily the truth that they are loved, valued, capable, and significant. If I do this, they will reach adulthood with a true concept of who they are. If I shirk this responsibility, I am leaving it up to my child to figure it out for him/her self. The likelihood is, they will not."

Dr. Smith goes on to say, "Whatever I tell them through my actions and words will be the truth for them, even if it is a lie."

If adults are to make successful attempts to help youth who are caught up in the lifestyle of selling drugs or some other dysfunctional behavior, the youth may need to understand the lies that bind them to that pattern in order for them to accept the truth. That youth may have been programmed to believe that "The game is the way out," and "Being caught up in the system is a normal part of life." Another youth across town has been programmed to believe "College is grade 13," and "Working for and designing the system is a normal part of life." As a man thinketh in his heart, so is he...(Proverbs 23:7). If we teach the drug dealing youth about college and legitimate career opportunities, let us simultaneously assist that youth in unlearning what is untrue about the "trap." The "untrue" crew (the media, the illegal opportunity structures, etc.) are hard at work crafting and disseminating life destroying messages. We, those who work for the other team, must be just as vigilant at exposing the lies as we are at imparting the truth.

Pick Your Pain

"We must all suffer one of two things: the pain of discipline or the pain of regret or disappointment."

- John Rohn

One of the group series that I do for my cognitive restructuring and re-socialization program is entitled "Pick Your Pain." During this six - week group series, we address the various types of pain people face in their lives – productive pain or destructive pain. This week I will share with you the concept we cover in our first group in the series "The pain of sacrifice and discipline versus the pain of the consequences of seeking instant gratification."

According to experts in neuroscience and psychology, (Joseph, 1999 & Smith, 2000), what people observe and how people are treated during the formative years can plant positive and/or negative beliefs in their minds without their knowing it. Many individuals are raised in environments where they are not taught the importance of sacrifice and discipline. They observe others around them seeking instant gratification by taking "short-cuts" and engaging in "get rich quick" schemes. At the same time, they are constantly exposed to movies, songs, commercials, and videos hailing praises for the "easy way" to get what one desires. The messages are clear: "You can sell drugs with no consequences and get rich quick," or "You can eat anything you want and be happy and healthy," or "You can have sex with the person you met at the club last night with zero consequences." The negative consequences are well documented and demonstrated in the lives of people who have bought into the lies, but the consequences are normalized. For example, prison and early death, which are consequences of participating in the "get rich quick" schemes classified as "The game," are normalized by the same rappers that proclaimed one can sell drugs with no consequences; but – for some reason – our young people do not get it.

Many of them are buying into the lie that the "game is the way out of poverty." The Reward: a few months or a couple years of "having it going on" aka "hood rich." The Pain: prison for 10 years, 20 years; a lifetime felon label, or death. In the meantime, other young people are internalizing and embracing the belief that "Higher education is the way out of poverty." The Pain: four, six, or eight years reading, studying, sleepless nights, working and going to school. The Reward: financial freedom, independence, a sense of accomplishment, being paid to do something you would do free.

Exercising for one hour a day five to six days a week along with healthy eating for six days a week and having one cheat day a week can completely alter a person's physical appearance and health. Unfortunately, unhealthy eating is not only promoted and marketed with no mention of the consequences, it has been labeled as a part of "our culture" in the African-American population.

The media that promote "easy sex" and "multiple relationships" as a lifestyle choice rarely discuss the pain after the thrill. The Reward: feeling good for a few minutes. The Pain: sexually transmitted diseases, teenage pregnancy, rejection, low self-esteem. Being selective, waiting, committing, has its own pain; but the rewards are awesome! The Rewards: a loving, caring, committed relationship. Noted poet Samuel Johnson put it this way,

"Pleasure that is obtained by unreasonable and unsuitable cost, must always end in pain."

What Type of Esteem Do You Have?

"Low self-esteem is like driving through life with your hand-break on."

- Maxwell Maltz

It is easy to proclaim that one has SELF-esteem, but life has a way of assisting you in determining where your true source of value lies. Many individuals have esteem that is dependent on external conditions and rooted in unconscious lies. Positive and/or negative unconscious beliefs (negative beliefs are also referred to as lies) are implanted in the unconscious mind by what people observe and how they are treated during the formative years (Joseph, 1999 & Smith, 2000). Say a person was raised in an environment in which he/she observed others being treated with dignity and respect based on their ownership of cars, fine clothes, and other material possessions that rapidly depreciate in value. Say that same person was taunted in school because he/she did not have the latest outfits, the "freshest" gym shoes, and the newest gadgets and toys, but witnessed others that possessed those items being treated as if they were valuable human beings. That person, more than likely, would have internalized the lie "An individual's value as a person is directly proportionate to the amount of material possessions they own." The media and makers of "toys" ensure that message is reiterated constantly.

Unfortunately, many people have CAR-esteem, CLOTHES-esteem, THIS IS MY MAN-esteem, THIS IS MY WOMAN-esteem, PERFECTLY SHAPED BODY-esteem, or EVERYBODY WANTS TO BE AROUND ME BECAUSE I GOT IT GOING ON-esteem. The reality of their external value system is not revealed until their supply is cut off. That is why many young men and women have legal problems today. They were trying to fund their esteem habit. External esteem is expensive, energy draining, and the acquisition process is time consuming.

The material possessions issue has a partner lie, "What other people think is more important than what I know to be true." People who do not have SELF-esteem may make decisions based on their need to have others think well of them. For example, they might spend their basic needs money on an outfit or on their nails because they want others to <u>THINK</u> they have it "going on." In that case, they have WHAT OTHER PEOPLE THINK ABOUT

ME-esteem. Many individuals make life-alternating decisions based on the need to feel important and valued. It is hard to transition from one environment where one's source of esteem is valued to another world where it is considered a bad investment; but in many cases that is exactly what is necessary to turn the light on. In some environments, spending all your money on clothes and gym shoes is considered foolish. Having one's external supply of validation cut off can make a person begin the REAL work of building true self-esteem. Unfortunately, in many cases, it makes some people advance to more destruction actions in order to "cop."

What Other People Think...OPP
Other People's Property

"To go against the dominant thinking of your friends, of most of the people you see every day, is perhaps the most difficult act of heroism you can perform."

- Theodore H. White

A lie that many people struggle with is "What other people think is more important than what I know to be the truth." Yet people, who struggle with that issue the most, staunchly declare, "I don't care what anybody thinks about me!" I speak of this issue with authority because I suffered with it most of my life. Although I have been delivered from this lie for the most part, on any given day, if I am not spiritually fit, I still struggle. Over the past years, I have worked intensively with people who have many issues and it has been my finding that this lie is very common and very deadly.

Dr. R. Joseph, noted expert in the fields of neuroscience and psychology, argues that adults make decisions, whether positive or negative, based on unconscious programming they received during the formative years. In adulthood, these beliefs are constantly accessed and make decisions for people without their conscious awareness (Joseph, 1992). Many individuals were raised in environments in which they witnessed people making decisions based on a desire to transmit a certain perception to others that was not necessarily true. For example, they may have witnessed adults around them spending all their money trying to make others THINK they had money but were poor and getting poorer by the minute. They may have watched someone act as if they knew a particular thing that they know absolutely nothing about, but they wanted others to THINK they possessed that information.

In adulthood, the person that has been unconsciously programmed to believe, "What other people think is more important than what I know to be the truth," will often make life altering decisions based on what they do or do not want other people to THINK. For example, a person may need to focus on school because God told them they are assigned to affect change in a particular industry that requires certain credentials. That person may want their "friends" to THINK they have not forgotten where they came from and are still "cool," so they hang out at their "friend's" barbecue when they should be studying, or they take their "friend's" two-hour phone call about absolutely nothing when they should be writing a paper. The lie-afflicted person ends up on academic probation, loses their financial aid, and now has PLENTY of time to hang out with their "friends" unfulfilled, purposeless, and angry. They may harbor resentments with their "friends" when in all actuality the culprit is the lie.

This lie "What other people think is more important than what I know to be the truth" has put many people in the penitentiary. They did not want people to THINK they were a punk, so they did a person great bodily harm or took a person's life based on something that person said. Young women have altered the entire course of their lives because they did not want people to THINK they were a prude so they gave in to the peer pressure trap of unwed, unprotected sex. Many Christians are doing everything in their power to make church folks THINK they are doing the "Lord's work" while neglecting what God really told them to do – their Kingdom Assignment. As John F. Kennedy so eloquently put it, "Conformity is the jailer of freedom and the enemy of growth."

The truth is "What other people think is OPP – Other People's Property." You are powerless over the thoughts and perceptions of others. In fact, a good question to ask yourself is, "Why do I need to <u>TRY</u> to control other people's thoughts and perceptions of me?" Many times people are not thinking about you at all – they may be wondering if they left the iron on. In other instances, people are thinking the exact opposite of what your mind is telling you. In some cases, some people are thinking all the negative things you think they think about you and…SO WHAT! A major reason people worry and fret over the thoughts of others is because they unconsciously believe those people have some power to negatively or positively impact their lives in some manner. The truth is…people have the power you give them. I have learned to spend my time making sure I am doing those things that I have been commanded to do by God and letting people, who don't have a heaven or a hell to put me in, think what they want. I am not suggesting that we should not care about what we do or say or the perceptions our actions transmit to others. I am suggesting that if we are doing the right things for the right reasons, we should allow other people's thoughts to be exactly what they are – OPP – OTHER PEOPLE'S PROPERTY!

Putting Unrealistic Expectations on Ourselves and Others

"We love to expect, and when expectation is either disappointed or gratified, we want to be again expecting."

- Samuel Johnson

A statement in the main text of a particular 12-Step program stresses that one of the biggest stumbling blocks to recovery is that we tend to put unrealistic expectations on ourselves and others. I am the type that reads a statement such as that, and I marinate on the words. As I mulled over this statement in my mind, I thought back over my many failed attempts at recovery to see if there was validity in this statement. I am not the type to believe a statement simply because someone expressed it. After much self-analysis, I found the statement to be true for my life. Over the course of my work as an addiction counselor, I have found that statement to be true in the lives of many. I have developed a group concept to help others recognize this tendency and its debilitating effect both on the subject and the object of the subject's expectations. Allow me to share some of my findings with you.

One expectation that we tend to put on others is for them to protect us from OUR OWN issues. You may say, "Anneshia what are you talking about!" Well, I'm glad you asked. One of the issues I struggled with (in the past) was the feeling that I had to pay people to tolerate me. In the *Lies That Bind®* Program, we express this issue, as "I have to compensate for my presence with goods and services." Because I had that issue/lie implanted in my unconscious mind as a child, I obeyed its directives for a great deal of my adult life and called it "being too nice." I would often obey the lie's directive by paying people for allowing me to exist, and then I would be resentful with others because they had accepted my payment. Let me make it clearer. As a child, the only time I received any attention or validation was when I was doing something for someone or giving someone something. By the time I went to school, this issue was so engrained in my mind that I would approach children and instead of introducing myself and asking if they wanted to play, I would say, "Hi, I have some candy."

As an adult, I would offer to pick up the check at the restaurant – all the time – despite the fact that I was not in a financial position to do so. At the movies, I would offer to pay the admission fee and buy the popcorn. That is dysfunctional in and of itself but what made matters worse was that I would drive home resentful and angry because the person I had "paid" to tolerate me had allowed me to pay. Most of the times, I had of my own free will called a person I knew was selfish, self-centered, and known for manipulating others and asked them if they wanted to go out. What did I expect them to say other than the usual "I don't have any money." Then I would offer to pay for everything, even though I was not in the position to do so. It was unrealistic for me to expect them to say, "Anneshia, PLEASE think about what you are offering. Can you really afford to do this? Anneshia, maybe we can put this off to another time when I have money. Anneshia, I like you for you and require nothing from you but for you to be you! Anneshia, I usually manipulate people, but I'm going to control that character defect simply because I know you do not have the wherewithal to protect yourself from other people's issues." That was an unrealistic expectation on my part. Later, I would sit at home broke and dissatisfied and feel hurt, lonely, rejected, used, inadequate, worthless and so forth. I was dissatisfied because I wanted to socialize with someone and enjoy interacting, but the entire evening was spent nursing and rehearsing the fact that the person was only there because I was paying for everything.

An unrealistic expectation that I put on myself for years was to be perfect and to do everything perfectly. As a child, those were expectations that were placed on me. Because the lies "You have to be perfect" and "You have to get it right the first time" were transmitted during my FORMATIVE YEARS, they were embedded in my unconscious mind. As an adult, I would experience frustration, self-loathing, and feelings of inadequacy, guilt, and shame when I could not meet those unrealistic expectations. If you pay close attention to the feelings that I listed from the unrealistic expectations that I put on others and myself, it is clear to see why this tendency is a stumbling block to recovery (recovery from any addiction). I sought relief from the pain in drugs, alcohol, food – and other mind and mood altering substances and/or activities. Please note that I only discuss two unrealistic expectations in this article to expose this issue, but I have a long list.

Let me share a few unrealistic expectations that people put on others all the time. (1) People expect others to have the same information they have, and if they don't, they consider those persons to be "stupid." (2) People expect others to acquire a skill in two weeks that took them years to develop. (3) People expect others to conquer a habit immediately, but they have been struggling with a habit for years that they have not even considered addressing. (4) People expect others to read their minds because they lack the self-confidence to articulate their needs. (5) People expect others to be good at the same things they are good at – to have the same forte. These are just a few we identify in my group and coaching sessions.

Let me share with you a few unrealistic expectations that people put on themselves. (1) They expect themselves to be perfect. (2) They expect themselves to mature in an area overnight. (3) They expect themselves to be strong all the time. (4) They expect themselves to bounce back from devastating events overnight. (5) They expect themselves to learn something in one week that it took their professor 20 years to master. (6) They expect themselves to live up to the expectations of others. The list goes on.

How do I address these issues? Glad you asked. The way I address these tendencies is by unearthing the lies supporting the unrealistic expectation, then telling myself the truth. I then assume my personal responsibilities in the situations – such as protecting myself from manipulators, expressing my needs to others, taking myself to the movies, associating with people who like me for me, and so forth. It is important to understand that it is not wrong to have expectations for yourself and for others but it is dysfunctional to have unrealistic expectations. It is also self-defeating to put expectations on others who have demonstrated that they are not interested in your expectations and/or do not have the capacity to meet them.

When I was a child, I talked as a child, "I have some candy. I'll pay your way to the movies and buy the popcorn." I thought as a child. I thought I had to pay people to act as if they liked me; I thought I had to accept abuse without question; I thought everyone was more important than I was. I reasoned as a child. My reasoning was, If I give people stuff, they will love me. If I accept abuse from people, they will eventually see how much I love them and stop hurting me. If I make people's needs and desires more important than mine, they will see how much I am willing to sacrifice to be with them and they will love me and return my kindness. Now that I am an adult (a mature woman of God), I have put away childish things. I have people in my life that like Anneshia for Anneshia and nothing more. They have their own resources, and we enjoy each other's company. I refuse to accept any type of abuse from any person. I take the needs of others into consideration, but you can best believe Anneshia's needs are met first, which allows me to do for others with a good spirit. I Corinthians 13:11 (Darby Translation), "When I was a child, I spoke as a child, I felt as a child, I reasoned as a child; when I became a man, I had done with what belonged to the child."

Was It the Trap or the Cheese - What's Your Cheese?

"The fox condemns the trap, not himself"

- William Blake

I have often heard the question asked, and I ask the question in my youth groups, "Was it the trap or the cheese that got the mouse?" We say, "It was the cheese." Now, some may say that is not a fair assessment. The poor little mouse had no awareness that the delight it sought was connected to its doom, and that is true to a certain extent. Here is the point we make in my group when we say it was the cheese. The mouse was focusing on what it wanted so much that it was not aware of what was connected to its desire. I am sure that there has been a time when a trap has snapped on the neck of a mouse, and the trap and mouse were not immediately removed from the vicinity. In that case, the other mice had the opportunity to witness the dead mouse caught in the trap. In addition, I am sure there has been a time when several mice were going after the cheese together. One got caught, and the others saw it. I wonder if the mice decided to get the cheese by crawling over the dead mouse. Things that make you go mmmmmmmm!

Now let's bring this home to people. How many times do we go after our "cheese," knowing that it is connected to a "trap?" You may say, "Anneshia, I went after that "cheese" with no awareness that it was connected to a trap." We may believe you the first time or two you got snapped in the "trap," but eventually one would start wondering how many times you are going to claim ignorance. The problem here is not so much the "trap" as it is the "cheese." What is your "cheese" that makes the jaws of the trap invisible until they snap shut around your neck? I know what my "cheese" was, and I know what my current "cheese" is – I am not confused. I attend "cheese" rehab daily – The Word of God renews my mind about the "cheese!"

Some people's "cheese" is the validation of others. Because of early childhood influences some people have unfinished business with certain types of people. Dr. R. Joseph (1992), noted expert in the fields of neuroscience and psychology, argues that because of unconscious influences from our childhood, some people seek out people and experiences that create the same not ok emotional atmosphere that was an earlier part of their existence. The doctor says there are two reasons we do this, (1) because it is familiar, and the familiar is easier to accept than what is unfamiliar, even if painful and (2) because we have an unconscious child that has some unfinished business with the types of people who hurt him or her – the child wants to "fix the script." The child is seeking to change the last scene. For years, my "cheese" was trying to win love and approval from emotionally unavailable people. My mother was never there for me emotionally as a child – I went through all sorts of changes trying to win her love and acceptance, and I never got it – THE END. For years, I sought out emotionally unavailable people trying to make them love and accept me. I went through all sorts of changes, trying to get their love and acceptance. They would act as if they loved and accepted me ("cheese") until they had gotten what they wanted, and then came the rejection, hurt, and abandonment ("trap"). What was so amazing about this equation is that I would return to the same people repeatedly, seeking love and acceptance "the cheese" after they had previously pulled the "bait and switch." My problem was not "the trap," it was the "cheese." Guess what, it was the "blind-mind syndrome." The god of this world has blinded the minds of the unbeliever - II Corinthians 4:4.

Some people's "cheese" is the so-called "easy way out" or the "get rich quick" scheme. Their "cheese" is seeking the reward without the labor. That is why so many young men and women are in prison today. They could not see the "trap," because they were looking at the "cheese." They listen to rap music talking about the "cheese." They watch videos with people dancing with the "cheese." Many people are in prison for their second or third "trap snap," and guess what; they are going after the "cheese" again when they get out! They are sitting in prison right now talking about the "cheese" and how they are going to "weave" next time instead of "bob," or "bob" next time instead of "weave." The makers of the trap have a "bob trap" and a "weave trap." They do not understand that they need to stop "bobbing and weaving" and renew their minds as it relates to the "cheese." By the way, there are people who have stopped getting their necks snapped, because they now get their "cheese" needs met making music that gets others to focus on the "cheese" instead of the "trap." What's up with that? Why not make "trap" videos and songs. Oh, that's right...they do make "trap" videos and songs. The makers of the "trap" are so confident that they can "cheese-matize" people that they now have songs calling it a "trap" while they show pictures of the "cheese" and people are still getting snapped.

A final point I want to make is that it is a compliment that a "trap" exists. Jeffrey Rubin wrote a book (1981) called "Psychological Traps." I read about his work in Psychology Today. He states that a "trap" has a purpose. "A trap allows hunters to outwit their quarry, to offset any advantage that the quarry may have by virtue of its greater power, speed, or the limited destructive capacity of the hunter's weapons. An animal trap accomplishes these ends in a strikingly simple and cleaver way: it brings the quarry to the hunter rather than the other way around." The fact that a trap exists means that the creator of the "trap" thinks you have some form of advantage "greater power or speed," and that their weapons have "limited destructive power." Therefore, a "trap" needs to be set to give them an advantage. However, understand the final point Mr. Rubin makes about the trap, "...it brings the quarry to the hunter rather than the other way around." Guess how it does that? I bet you can't guess! Right – IT'S THE "CHEESE!"

Renew your mind – Romans 12:1-2 – that's how I changed my thinking. John 8:32 say, "And ye shall know the truth, and the true shall set you free!" If knowing the truth will set you free, it MUST be a lie that has you bound. The "cheese" is a lie – an illusion. Dr. Martin Luther King Junior put it this way, “Freedom is never voluntarily given by the oppressor; it must be demanded by the oppressed.” Read the Word and stop being “cheese-matized” – demand your freedom!

Unspoken Lies = Articulated Invalidation!

"The naked truth is always better than the best dressed lie."

- Ann Landers

Throughout my years of work exposing unconscious lies, it has been my experience that not only do people mistreat themselves based on the "Lies That Bind®," they also accept maltreatment from others based on the lies. Allow me to explain. If a person acts as if they have certain rights and privileges but treats you as if you are not entitled to those same rights and privileges, then they are saying something. If a person makes a mistake and chalks it up to being human, but acts as if you are a horrible, pitiful excuse of a human being for making a mistake, that person is saying something. That person is saying that they are entitled to certain rights and privileges (being human, making mistakes) for which you are not entitled. They are saying that you have to live up to their unrealistic expectations and standards, but they are exempt from those same expectations and standards for some unarticulated reason. So what should you do about this? Undress the lie – articulate the unarticulated lie. For example, if someone goes off on you because you forgot to pick up the dry cleaning once, then that person is saying:

- You have to be perfect.
- You have to do everything perfectly.
- You have to be 100% at all times in every situation.
- Failure to live up to my standard of perfection means that you are a despicable human being and should be ashamed of yourself.

Now that same person who is communicating these unspoken lies makes mistakes all the time. In fact, they forgot to take the garbage out last week, and you had to put the garbage in the car and chase the garbage truck. That same person forgot to get milk when they went to the store, and milk was the reason they went to the store in the first place. When they make mistakes, they are entitled to do so because they are a human being and human beings make mistakes. The indignation they expressed when you forgot to pick up the dry-cleaning articulated the lies. The way they expect to be treated when they make a mistake, in combination with the unspoken lies, communicates the invalidation of you. Let me provide another example.

Let's say a certain person was raised in an environment in which they were taught certain principles such as the importance of education, how to eat healthy and exercise, how to express love and concern for others. Their adult life reflects what they were taught as a child. If another person was raised in an environment in which this other person was taught that education was not important, to eat unhealthy food and avoid physical activities, that love was assumed not demonstrated – that person's adult life now reflects what they were taught. If the person raised in the healthy environment treats the person raised in the unhealthy environment as if they were stupid or despicable for not possessing information they were not taught, that person is saying something. That person is saying that the person who was raised in the unhealthy environment:

- Is expected to automatically know things they were not taught.
- Is stupid
- Is not capable of learning positive things

Now if the person raised in the healthy environment was a social worker and they had to take a high-level statistic class in their PhD program, they would not expect the professor to act as if they should possess that information simply because he or she (the professor) does. In fact, they would be indignant and call the dean if the professor treated them as if he or she expected them to know statistics automatically, or if the professor treated them as if they were stupid for not having information he or she (the professor) internalized over the course of 25 years. Get my point?

So, undress the lies. When people act as if you should possess information automatically because they do, but unapologetically say, "I did not know that" when they are introduced to new information – call them out. Say something like, "So I'm expected to know things automatically that it took you years to internalize but you have a right to NOT know things and be taught what you do not know. Wow, tell me how to get those human rights that you possess!"

> **Warning:** If you are in a relationship with a violent person, you may want to say that to yourself, in your head, and consult with a domestic violence program for an exit strategy.

Let me give you one more example that I am sure will make the manipulators of the world very angry☺.

If a person acts as if the only time they have any use for you is when you are giving them something or doing something for them, then that person is saying something. That person is saying, "I'm important – you are unimportant. I am only tolerating you. You have to pay me with goods and services in order for me to put up with you for small increments of time – and the meter is running. If you have nothing to give me, or if you are not in a position to do something for me, then you are of zero value to me." Now that same person who expects payment for their presence acts as if you are crazy if you ask them to do ANYTHING for you or give you ANYTHING. Undress the unspoken lies and the articulated invalidation. You can say it like this, "So, you are saying that the only time that you are able to "tolerate" me is when I am doing something for you or giving you something. At the same time, I am out of my mind if I ask you to do something for me or give me something – is that what you are saying?" Hear me WRGO readers, if a person leaves your life because you will no longer tolerate A,B,C (A,B,C is whatever you will no longer tolerate), then you must face the fact that they were only in your life for A,B,C in the first place. All you have lost if they leave is someone who was using you for A,B,C! That has everything to do with them and their defects of character and nothing to do with you and your value as a person.

Refuse to tolerate the lies that the enemy is using to bind you. Call them out. Knowing the truth will set you free, but exposing the lie is just as important. As Shapley R. Hunter puts it, "The continued utterance of a lie does not make it true, but it does convince many that it is, particularly if you can squelch most efforts to expose the lie."

The Trust Factor

"It is an equal failing to trust everybody, and to trust nobody."

- English Proverb

A common statement that I hear in my work as a counselor is, "I don't trust anyone!" This statement is usually based on past experiences with untrustworthy, deceitful people. My response to those who tell me they do not trust anyone is that their trust issue is with themselves – not others. When you are able trust yourself to follow certain principles, you do not have to spend a great deal of time worrying about trusting people.

I learned that, in the past, the reason I had so many issues with trust was because I was not taught certain principles. If I had been taught, as Maya Angelou says, to believe people when they show me who they are, I would not have had so many issues with trust. For example, there have been times, before I began participating in cognitive restructuring, when I would listen to a person as they discussed other people's personal business with me for hours. Then, for some strange reason, I would share something deep and personal with that person. It would be my sincere desire and expectation that this person would not repeat the contents of the conversation with anyone. Later when I found out that the known gossiper had spread my business all over town, I was hurt, indignant, and angry. I would then irately declare, "You can't trust people! That's why I don't do people!" In reality, the person that could not be trusted in this situation was me. At that point in my life, I could not trust myself to be observant of the issues that others display and position myself accordingly. The gossiper I told my personal business to **could** be trusted. She could be trusted to do what she always did when given information – TELL IT! I now trust and believe gossipers when they show me who they are.

Let me share another example of my inability to trust myself. In the past, I could not trust myself to get to know a person before giving them a "front row seat" in my life. There were times when I met a man, and one week later, he was assigned the label of "significant other." Three weeks after that, I was in the fetal position feeling hurt, indignant, and angry. Was the issue with the man or me? He was untrustworthy, but I had not given him time to SHOW me who he was. I believed his representative with no investigation or prudence on my part. It is not as if he was going to introduce himself by saying,

"Hello madam, I am an untrustworthy fellow. I would like to get to know you, and given the opportunity, I will horribly violate you as I have countless others." History has demonstrated to me time and time again that most people send their representative to the table for the first few weeks or months of a relationship. So WHY would I NOT protect myself by getting to know a person before allowing them access to my heart? Why would I not believe a person when they showed me they were a gossiper? The answer: I could not be trusted to protect myself.

Now that I have gotten to know and love myself, I am much more cautious of whom I allow in my inner circle. I am much more discerning of people. I have stopped being so arrogant as to assume that I am exempt from being victimized by a negative trait someone has demonstrated they possess. Meaning, if I know that a person is a gossiper, I only discuss things with them that I do not care if they repeat – such as the weather or the price of gas. I no longer assume that just because a person who suffers with a certain defect of character has not gotten me YET, that they will not "do me" given the chance. YET, stands for You're Eligible Too." When I meet a man that I may be interested in getting to know better, I put on my private detective hat. Oh, yes, the Investigation Discovery Channel does not have anything on me. That may sound rigid to some, but as I learned to love myself and as I began accumulating sweat-equity in my station in life; I became much more prudent about my choices as they relate to who I allow in my life and the content of our conversations.

My lessons on trust do not exempt me from making mistakes as they relate to people. No matter how careful a person is, they can still be "taken for a ride" from time to time. Even in those types of situations, I have learned to trust myself. I trust myself to end the connection once I discover I made a bad choice. I trust myself to not take the character flaws of others personally. I trust myself to end the association without judging the person too harshly, realizing that I have character flaws of my own. I trust myself to say "note to self" rather than berate myself for making a judgment error. I trust myself to stand on the promises in the Word such as "No weapon formed against me shall prosper."

The wisdom contained in the protection strategies expressed in this article is not my own. God gave this wisdom to me. I trust God, and I trust the lessons that He has taught me through my experiences. As an extra bonus, the principles in this article help me in my love walk (which still needs some work). It is much easier to love a manipulator who is not given the opportunity to manipulate me. It is much easier to love a gossiper who does not have access to information I do not want publicly known. Trust is possible when accompanied by certain principles.

The "Land of Should" Versus the "Is Case"

"A man should look for what is,
and not for what he thinks should be"

- Albert Einstein

My undergrad *Consumer Service Strategies* professor taught our class a very powerful principle. He dedicated an entire session to the "should versus is" concept. He articulated this notion while describing how to deal with a customer complaint. My professor stated, "Many people respond to situations with a "should be" mentality instead of approaching circumstances with a mindset to address the "Is Case" first. He expressed that if a customer comes to the complaint department and says, "a, b, c... happened, and I'm upset about it," we should not spend ten minutes telling him/her what "should" have happened. He stated the customer usually knows what SHOULD have happened – that is why they are at the complaint window in the first place.

What my Professor taught the class is a principle that I have found to be applicable in my daily life. He taught us that we must first deal with what "Is" going on before we have a right to enter the "Land of Should." My instructor did not say we should never look at a situation and envision what should be – quite the contrary. He taught us that in order to properly manifest the vision, we have to deal with the "Is Case" (the current conditions) so that we can determine what and where Point A is in order to create the roadmap to Point B – what should be. Here are a few, practical, real life examples of this principle in action.

There are times that I have said to a person "Why did you do that to me? You SHOULD not treat people like that!" I was living in the "Land of Should." I was "shoulding" on myself. The fact of the matter is that the person I was talking to had already demonstrated to me through word, action, and deed that he/she had no problem treating people in a manner that I classified as unacceptable. They were probably thinking SHOULD too. They were probably thinking, "You SHOULD find a person who shares your principles and standards for relationships if you have a problem with my philosophies. Since you are not dealing with the "Is Case" as it relates to me, I will deal with the "Is Case" as it relates to you. You "Is" choosing to continue to associate with me even though I have shown you who I am, so I will continue to be me and do what I do. How about that!"

Another example of this principle in operation is seen in the Human Service Industry in how certain social programs operate. It is my belief that programs that are supposed to address social ills SHOULD actually do what they claim they do. The "Is Case" is that some programs do what they say they do – help people – and in those situations the "Is" and the "Should" are matching. In other programs the "Should" and the "Is" are not corresponding. If we go around "shoulding" on society (spending hours upon hours talking about what SHOULD be happening), the problems will continue to exist while we simply talk. The only way things will change – truly change, is if we cop to the "IS CASE" (Point A) and develop a plan to address the current state of affairs. Here is how we can do this...how about we begin by admitting, "This program says it is doing "a,b,c," and it has the capacity to do "a,b,c," but in actuality there are some issues with the program that are producing an "e,f,g" result." Since we have identified the "IS CASE" instead of acting as if IS and SHOULD are synonymous, we are now able to formulate a plan to address the "IS CASE." After addressing the issues, we can begin working on the vision to operationalize the SHOULD capacity of the program.

The process I just described sounds simple doesn't it; well it is not that simple. It has been my experience that many individuals have an aversion to dealing with the "Is Case," because it makes people uncomfortable to admit that what they claim is happening is not really happening. Another issue is that the "Is Case" is not adversely affecting them. Others will not speak up because of some unconscious need to "fit in" or be accepted by the mainstream. If society is to move to the next level in addressing social ills, some people have to take a stand. Changes can be actualized over time if people are willing to endure the process associated with true transformation. Arthur Schopenhauer brilliantly described the process when he said, "New truths go through three stages. First they are ridiculed, second they are violently opposed, and then, finally, they are accepted as self-evident."

A Place Called Go!

"A year from now you may wish you had started today."

- Karen Lamb

In January of 2001, I began my academic journey at Grand Rapids Community College (GRCC). At the time I was living in a recovery house and talking about my education plans at a well known 12-Step Program of which I am a member. There were times when people would hear me talk about my challenges, successes, and struggles at school and approach me afterwards and say, "You know Anneshia, I've been thinking about going back to college. You have really inspired me." Well it is 2011. I am one semester away from completing my second master's degree on a future faculty fellowship. Some of the people who approached me in 2001 have gone to college and are working in their careers and pursuing other academic goals, but many of the people who approached me are still "thinking" about going back to school. They have not become acquainted with "A Place Called Go!"

There is a point in life when we must stop "thinking" and "talking" about something and DO something. We often hear the saying, "The longest journey begins with a single step." That is so true. There was "Day One" when I walked onto the campus of GRCC (a single step) fearful, nervous, unsure, insecure, and doubtful. I was at "A Place Called Go!" How I felt was irrelevant. I was there! I did not get there by myself. The Director of the recovery house I lived in had told me and the other residents in no uncertain terms that we must work, volunteer, or be in school. She told us that we were not "disabled" when we were smoking crack so we would not be "disabled" in her house. I was not a lazy person but I needed someone to shout GO to encourage me to push pass the fear, uncertainty, and insecurity.

Too many people are "stretching." When I say stretching, I mean they are saying things like "I believe the Lord is saying that I should go back to school" or "I've been thinking that maybe I should lose some weight" or "I believe I should get out of this dysfunctional relationship." That is "stretching." While they are "stretching," the start gun has fired 12 times. Other people are running past them going to college, opening businesses, going to the gym five times a week, and enjoying healthy relationships. Many of the people who are "making things happen" are not children of light – some people are doing this in the dark. Come on children of light – GO! This is the only life you have. This is not a dress rehearsal. This is the real deal! I am preaching to myself as well. Although I am "getting it in" in certain areas, there are some places where I need to GO also. Let's GO together. When you see me say, "GO Anneshia," and when I see you I will say, "GO!" Do not let your past accomplishments be the deterrent to your next level. A wise man once said, "Some people's minimums are other people's maximums." Do not allow a person who does not have your capacity determine how well you are doing. If you are an eagle, check in at eagle camp and see how they "get down!"

Another point I must make is, do not run to the next level poorly trained for battle. That is not what "A Place Called Go" means. "A Place Called Go" is about doing what you need to do on each level, and when you have completed the necessary tasks on one level, GOING on to the next level and doing what needs to be done there. I could not have gone to the master's program until I had completed the bachelor's program. I needed to be conditioned on one level to write three page papers, then six page papers, then 15 page papers in order to be ready to write 25 and 30 page papers in which each section had to meet stringent criteria. Level One –GO! You have now completed Level One – advance to Level Two. Level Two – GO! You have now completed Level Two, advance to Level Three – GO! The next few years are going to go by whether you are doing what you said you were going to do or not.

This week's column is not for everyone. This column is for individuals who have fire shut up in their bones – fire that demands credentialing. Do not allow the enemy to lull you to sleep with his lie, "Talk very profoundly about the situation, but take no action to change anything." Refuse to continue "stretching," talking about what you believe God is telling you to do. Do it! Stop talking profoundly, quoting Bible versus, and shouting around the church about something you are not doing – GET IT IN! The kingdom of darkness is getting it in. We can do all things...through WHO! Come on now! If the kingdom of darkness has a doctor on duty (WHO GOT IT IN) doing unnecessary procedures on people to make money, then the kingdom of light should have a doctor on duty (WHO GOT IT IN) destroying the works of the enemy in that industry. As John F. Kennedy put it, "There are risks and costs to action. But they are far less than the long range risks of comfortable inaction."

The Comfort Zone

"It is *not because things are difficult that we do not dare, it is because we do not dare that things are difficult."*

- Seneca

I participate in a spin class (in-door biking) at the gym five times a week. After we have warmed up and are about to begin the real work, the instructor informs us that we are about to "push pass the comfort zone." The comfort zone is a place that one has adjusted to and is able to maintain a steady pace without pain or extra exertion. We return to the comfort zone from time to time (for 30 seconds or a minute) to revive (grab some water) and prepare for the next level. We are still moving and working in the comfort zone, but our heart rate has returned to normal, and we can articulate a sentence or two if we desire. When we are pushing ourselves, our total focus is on the work and listening to the instructions – there are no conversations. What I have noticed at spin class is that after we have worked for a while, the level that was once painful and uncomfortable becomes comfortable, and at that point, the instructor challenges us to find another level so we do not "cheat" ourselves.

In life, we often find ourselves in the "comfort zone." It is not that we have stopped working, but we have adjusted, and there is no need for extra exertion. The problem is that the next level requires a new intensity that will generate discomfort for a period. The "comfort zone" could be a job when we really desire a career. The "comfort zone" could be associations with people who have accepted mediocre as the standard when we really desire to interact with people who model excellence. The "comfort zone" could be a certain weight that is not unattractive, but not exactly what we want to see when we look in the mirror. The career, the new group of friends, the desired body weight are on the other side of our discomfort. Why do we often find it so hard to FEEL uncomfortable for a period of time in order to achieve what we truly want in life?

My challenge to myself and WRGO readers is to push ourselves the second part of the year to the next level. The new career may involve education, which will require the discomfort of study and testing. The new relationships with people of excellence (eagles) may require feeling awkward and uncertain. You might have to look up some words the "eagles" use when you get home at night, and you may have to call someone and ask what to wear to the event the "eagles" are hosting. The weight loss, the 15 pounds you are struggling to lose (Anneshia), will require discomfort while you train your appetite to adjust to a new level. The beauty of the process is that YOU WILL ADJUST TO THE NEW LEVEL then you must find a new challenge in a new area. As noted philosopher Simone de Beauvior puts it, "Life is occupied in both perpetuating itself and in surpassing itself. If all life does is maintain itself, then living is only not dying."

This...Is...Nothing

"Once you make a decision,
the universe conspires to make it happen."

- Ralph Waldo Emerson

During the second semester of my bachelor's degree coursework, I was taking a class entitled "Small Business Administration" in an accelerated format. I was also taking college algebra which was one of the most challenging classes – for me – of the four college degrees I possess. During that time, I had also just regained custody of one of my daughters who I had left when she was eight months old due to my dysfunctional lifestyle. She was 12.5 years old when she came home with me. I was also working fulltime. Life was challenging. The small business administration (SBA) class I was taking was offered in a seven-week accelerated format. We were expected to do four months worth of work in seven weeks. The university told the student body when they began offering classes in the seven-week format that some people would not be able to handle that format and it was up to us to "call the play" as to whether or not we had what it took to do that much work in that short of a time span. The overachiever, workaholic, performance issued person that I was at that time said, "What! Come on with it.!" Now the story gets interesting.

A core assignment for the SBA course was a business plan. During the seven weeks, we had to read four chapters a week, take a quiz on those chapters, write papers, and still have our business plan done by the end of the semester. We nontraditional students also had to maintain our work, family, and other coursework simultaneously. I was spending a great deal of time in the math lab because college algebra was "wiping the floor" with me. Our professor said he was not going to "crunch" the numbers in the financial section of the business plan, because he knew that many of us had not taken the corporate finance class yet. The week before the business plan was due; I had not even begun to work on the document or the PowerPoint presentation we had to do to present our plan. When we walked in the classroom, week six, we had a new professor. Our old professor, who was not going to "crunch" the numbers, was no longer working at the university. The new professor listed his extensive credentials and stated he was "crunching" numbers in our business plan that was due in one week.

As I sat in that chair, fear and doubt had a conversation with me. Those two demoniacs chastised me for having the nerve to think I could make it in any world other than the world I had walked away from a few years previously. Fear and doubt told me to give up and call-it-a-day. As I sat in the chair struggling through a destiny altering decision, I turned to the woman sitting next to me and asked her, "Do you have any of your business plan done?" The woman next to me was a person I did not particularly care for. In fact, I groaned when I walked in day one of class and saw her in my class – AGAIN! She was the type who kept the conversation with the professor going – ensuring we would be in class the entire four hours! At this point, I was "sinking" and did not care who had the "lifeboat." This woman was from Romania and had a very distinct accent. She looked me straight in my eyes sensing the importance of the moment – reading the fear and doubt. She said in her heavy accent, "I have NOTHING done! But I will have it all done next "week," and so will YOU!" My classmate from Romania looked at the books and papers in front of her with utter contempt and said, "THIS...IS...NOTHING!" I had never told her that I grew up in a torture chamber with Attila the Hun and Jack the Ripper. I had no idea what happened to her in Romania, but right then something powerful happened. Two women, who have both been to hell and back and had lived to tell the story, made a connection in the spirit realm. She knew I had seen hell, and I knew she had seen hell. What she was saying was, "I know you are not going to allow this little 20 to 30 page assignment punk you out and make you give up after all you have been through!" It was as if someone had injected me with determination and strength. I got up, went into the hallway – where other students were calling people saying they were taking days off work, asking people to baby-sit, and making plans to meet the challenge set before us – and started making my own plans.

That weekend – in two days – I GOT IT ALL DONE! I had forgotten that I had a degree in Computer Applications Technology and typed 100 wpm. Not only did I get the work done, I got "giggy" with it and did a commercial with animated clipart characters for my PowerPoint presentation. I went to Kinko's and had my business plan printed and bound with a high-glossy, laminated cover. The professor was impressed and so were my classmates. The three words that my classmate gave me that day helped me finish that class and have helped me complete my Bachelor's in Business Studies, my Master's in Business Administration, the education and experience hours for my certification for addiction counseling, and most recently, my Master's in Social Work!

I soared on her words for two years until God impressed upon me to do a word search on "nothing" in the Bible. I laughed so hard I almost cried when I saw the revelation He meant for me to have for future reference. Philippians 4:6-7 says that we are to be anxious for NOTHING, but we are to let our requests be known to God. It also denotes that if we follow this way, we will have peace. So now, whenever fear and doubt decide to talk to me, I thank them for writing my prayer list. Whatever is going on is NOTHING I should be worried about – it's something to pray about. As we know, faith without works is dead, so the next NOTHING God showed me was, Luke 10:19 – Amplified version. In this verse, God is saying that He has given us power and authority [physical and mental strength and ability] over **all** the power of the enemy, and that NOTHING can in any way harm us. So today, when things are coming against me, I keep working without taking "fear" breaks, because I know I have power and authority over them. I am not saying I do not feel fear at times, I simply mean I do not allow fear to stop me; and before I allow it to torment me for an extended period of time, I use the NOTHING principle.

Another NOTHING God pointed out is found in Luke 1:37. That verse states that with God, NOTHING is impossible. Therefore, whatever new venture I am walking into, whatever obstacle I need to obliterate – is NOTHING that is impossible for God to handle. Now the last NOTHING point is for the children of darkness who think they have the power to hinder the work of God by coming against his children. It plainly states in Isaiah 41:10-12, that God is with his children to help them. He says that those that come against His children will be as NOTHING. He called them NOTHING in verse 11 and verse 12. When I walk past people I know are being used of the enemy to try to stop me, I say to myself – "There is NOTHING you can do that is going to stop the work that God has ordained for my life."

Whatever is happening that is generating fear in your life, file it under <u>NOTHING</u> and do what God has commanded you to do about <u>NOTHING</u>. Do not fear it, pray about it, know you have authority and power over it, know that God can handle it, and it will fade away and be nonexistent. That SBA class faded away with an A!

They Made That Up – Let's Make Something Else Up!

"You must be the change
you wish to see in the world"

- Mahatma Gandhi

One of the slang expressions widely used in Detroit is "You made that up!" It is said with a certain vocal tone, voice inflection and body language – a certain swag per say. What that phrase means is, "You just made that up, hoping I would buy into it so you could benefit in some way at my expense – it's not going down!" Although that statement is primarily used in the context of the "game" (aka "the trap"), it is applicable to society in general.

Everything that exists today whether it is an invention, a concept, a theory, a rap song, an industry…someone MADE IT UP. Some of the entities and concepts that exist are beneficial to mankind and to the inventors we say, "THANK YOU – GOOD JOB!" Some of the entities and concepts that currently exist appear to be beneficial, but from a holistic and long-term perspective, they are racist, classist, and sexist. Someone MADE THOSE UP! Some of the concepts and entities that exist are overtly destructive. Someone MADE THOSE UP TOO! The people that "make" stuff up are innovators whether they work for the Kingdom of Light or the kingdom of darkness. They are leaders. *"Innovation distinguishes between a leader and a follower."* Steve Jobs

Instead of simply sitting around discussing, critiquing, and shaking our heads in dismay at the destructive ideologies and methodologies that are wrecking havoc on our children, families, communities, and nation, why don't we MAKE SOMETHING ELSE UP! We do not have to sit idly by allowing some profit seeking entity to deliver music to our children encouraging them to sell drugs, flaunt their bodies, and be a gangster without coming back at them just as strongly as they are coming at us! Let's make some rap music about the university, or designing a business (that doesn't profit off the destruction of another person), or creating a NEW industry! Hey, young rappers who claim you have lyrics; I am issuing you a challenge...SHOW US YOU CAN MAKE SOMETHING ELSE UP! Anybody can rap about the "trap," but can you rap about the "keys" to get out of the trap? Get the beat right, get the lyrics right, we will help you with the marketing strategy and GET PAID helping people! We do not have to keep falling for something someone "made up hoping we would buy into it so they could benefit in some way at our expense." Stand up and declare, "IT'S NOT GOING DOWN!"

This same principle applies to every industry in the world. If there are some things wrong in the human service industry – MAKE SOMETHING ELSE UP! We do not have to worship at the "shrine" of "best" practices as if that is as good as it gets. Best practice means that is the best we have so far. We do not have to throw the baby out with the bathwater but we can certainly scrutinize a concept to see what is working and distinguish it from what is being made to appear as if it is working. If there are some things that are not right in the medical industry – MAKE SOMETHING ELSE UP! If there are some things not right in the education system – MAKE SOMETHING ELSE UP! I am not suggesting we run on the battlefield poorly trained for battle. I am suggesting we do what we need to do to prepare: be prayerful, be creative, be dynamic, be strategic and MAKE SOMETHING ELSE UP! All of creation is moaning and groaning waiting on you. "Discovery consists of seeing what everybody has seen and thinking what nobody has thought." — Albert von Szent-Gyorgy

The Non-Negotiable Goal

"The more intensely we feel about an idea or a goal, the more assuredly the idea, buried deep in our subconscious, will direct us along the path to its fulfillment"

- Earl Nightingale

Last year I was asked to speak again at a large convention of a well-known, 12-Step Program in Detroit. As I always do, I prayed and asked God what He wanted me to share. Although my story does not change, there is much to my story, as I have been alive 47 years. God directed me through His spirit to do a comparative analysis of how I met goals when I was using drugs to how I meet goals today.

Before I begin, for the record, I would like to clarify that I am not proud of the life I lived when using drugs. Addiction is pure, unadulterated, double-jointed, bondage, and I thank GOD for delivering me from that torture chamber. Come with me into the daily routine of a crack addict seeking to fulfill a life-destroying, society-harming goal. The important aspect of the goal that annihilated all obstacles that stood between me and the attainment of the goal was one important criterion; the goal was "non-negotiable" – IT'S GOING DOWN; IT'S GOT TO HAPPEN! This is when the crack had become synonymous with oxygen in my life. What I am about to do in this article is demonstrate how the "non-negotiable" criterion makes the difference when pursuing a goal. This principle is transferable to life-enhancing, society- changing goals.

When I was using drugs, the opinions of others did not hinder me from the pursuit of the goal – not the non-negotiable goal. You see, I was the addict that the other addicts talked about. In the subculture I frequented in Detroit, they talk about people in the third person and change the gender. I had broken their code and understood when they were talking about me in the third person. They often would say things like, "If I ever get like that, I'll get me some help!" While they were talking, I was thinking. I was not thinking about what they were saying. I articulated my thoughts to them immediately after they voiced their assessment of my state, "Can I use your lighter?" You see my thoughts were on the goal, not people's assessments of my current condition. In my mind, what they were talking about was irrelevant because it was not goal related. Now, let's compare this to today. Do I focus on what others think about me and my current condition as I pursue my goal – My Kingdom Assignment? Whenever I start focusing on people's assessment of me, God reminds me of how unconcerned I was about what others thought about me when I was destroying my life. God often asks me why I am focusing on what others think of me who are in the same or a worse state as me, or have no goals at all. Focus on the goal, Anneshia, and keep it moving!

When I was using drugs, I was able to live by a budget and control my eating. There was only one thing on the budget – CRACK – but that was a budget I followed religiously. I remember walking past a restaurant in Detroit on Woodward Avenue one day with $30 in my pocket. My stomach was growling, screaming, begging, "Please!!! Feed me!!!!" I said, "No! Food is not on the budget today. You ate day before yesterday. You are not going to die if you don't eat right now. It's just a feeling – push through it." Now, let's compare that to my ability to live by a budget and monitor my eating today. Am I able to restrain myself from buying a pair of shoes or an outfit when it's not in the budget? Am I able to tell myself that feeling of hunger is just a feeling and I won't die when attempting to lose weight? Come on Anneshia! How could you be so focused and determined for a life-destroying goal and turn into super WIMP when pursuing a goal that will change your life and impact society for the good! I know how and why, the "get high" goal was non-negotiable so therefore any wants and feelings that were counterproductive to the goal were irrelevant. I am preaching to myself today. If this helps you, good!

The last point I want to make about active addiction was my ability to push past the fear and the obstacles to do what I needed to do. The streets of Detroit are very dangerous. There was a time when I worked the streets that a serial killer was stalking women. I was out there during the time when he killed 17 women. The women on the streets of Detroit rob other women on the streets. I often owed two to three dope crews large sums of money and had to spend a certain amount of money with each crew daily in order to keep them from calling in the loan. We often had "rookie-officer morality" on duty who was going to clean up the streets of Detroit single-handedly on his first day. The temperature was often below zero. I would be in my hotel room preparing for my day going over the obstacles I would face in my mind! I was thinking about the obstacles in a "solution-oriented" manner. Not once did I consider not going. The serial killer, "He just hasn't met the right one yet – I'm the right one dude!" The dope crews – I had a plan. "Rookie-officer morality" – I had a plan. The other women on the streets – I had a plan. The weather – I convinced myself it was not that bad. In fact, I rationalized two and three ways the weather was to my advantage.

Now you may ask, "Anneshia what happened if things did not go according to your plan?" Glad you asked! I would encourage myself, regroup, and go back to the drawing board. For instance, when "rookie-officer morality" arrested me, I encouraged myself all the way to the police station. I would say, "Anneshia you are tired. You need to rest anyway. You will be out tomorrow. Hang in there girl." When I was about to miss a payment deadline with one of the crews, and they jumped out the car on me, I would talk so fast and so convincingly (improvisation), they would not only let me go but sometimes increased the loan. I got beat up a few times but I accepted it as part of the process and kept it moving – limping down the road.

Let's summarize the principles. When the goal is non-negotiable, when it is synonymous with oxygen, you will do certain things. 1) Relegate your feelings to the category of irrelevant when they are counterproductive to the goal. 2) Feel the fear but don't let it stop you. 3). Make plans for obvious obstacles. 4) Improvisation/adaptation (as Morpheus told Neo). 5) Face disappointment and failure with an "assess, regroup, back to the drawing board" mentality. You see, the reason I could live by those principles when I was using drugs was simply because the goal, "the temporary absence of pain," was non-negotiable. Today, my prayer is that God helps you and I internalize the "non-negotiable" factor of our Kingdom Assignment on this earth. Life becomes an adventure with that component in place. As Jim Rohn puts it, "We must be careful not to let our current appetites steal away any chance we might have for a future feast."

The "I Do That Too" Principle

"Everything that irritates us about others can lead us to an understanding of ourselves."

\- Carl Jung

God often provides me with "training simulations" to assist me on my road to spiritual maturity. One of the principles that He has taught me is the "I do that too" principle. I also refer to it as the "I do that too" gift. This principle greatly inhibits me from indulging in one of my emotional drugs of choice which is indignation. Let me clarify. In traffic someone may cut me off, and my very spiritual response has often been, "You idiot! You saw me! You did that on purpose! Where did you get your license...the cereal box?" Then moments later, I cut someone off, accidentally of course, and they blew their horn loudly and gave me the finger or a dirty look. My response then was "I did not see you. It was an accident. You didn't have to blow your big, scary horn at me (sniff)." There is an old saying that states, "We tend to judge others by their actions, and we judge ourselves by our intentions." My first reaction was to categorize the person's actions that cut me off in traffic as a sinister plot rather than an accident; while moments later I did the exact same thing and immediately classified my actions as an innocent mistake. The rest of the way to my destination I received a lecture from God on my tendency to give myself the benefit of the doubt while criminalizing others. I am not suggesting that people do not at times cut others off in traffic on purpose. I am suggesting we need to stop being so hard on others and so soft on ourselves; realizing that most of what we judges others for...WE DO THAT TOO!

Allow me to share another example. There are times when I have been horribly upset because others have passed judgment on me with little to no information. I have put my halo on and "smoked" what I deemed as "righteous" indignation. In all actuality, I have done the EXACT same thing many times. I have judged someone with little to no information or with information from a third-party who I knew drank "hatorade" on a regular basis. Although I have been granted the "I do that too" gift, my automatic response system at times still defaults to using an "unjust weight" as I interact with others; but the gift voids the transaction. As a certified alcohol and drug counselor, I have witnessed people get hurt or angry, and return to active use after a period of clean time based on something someone did to them that they did to someone else the week before.

Even though it still hurts when I find out that someone is harshly judging me based on my past, as I am a human being, I now use the gift of "I do that too" and skip the indignation. Now I say to myself when I encounter someone judging me based on the fact that I used drugs in the past, "Well maybe a person addicted to drugs really hurt them or is still hurting them. Maybe that's why they have trouble with my past. I have been hurt in various ways in my childhood, and I have issues accepting people who disclose that they have hurt children in the past, but have changed." That is not to say that people are right for judging me or that I have a right to judge others as Matthew 7:1 says "Judge not, that ye be not judged." The reality is that I still struggle with being completely nonjudgmental, and most people I have encountered on my journey struggle too.

I use this concept in one of my groups. I have everyone make a list of the things people do that irritate them and the things that people do that hurt them. Then I asked them to review the list and circle the things they do on the list. If they do not do any of the things on the list, I challenge them to identify some irritating and hurtful things they do or have done to others. One of the things that comes up quite often is being hurt when they find out that others are talking negatively about them. Most people, who identify this as hurtful, cannot look me in the eye and say they do not or have not ever talked negatively about someone. The gift of "I do that too" allows you to gain control over your emotions, stay off the pity-pot, forgive others more easily, and if nothing else – it helps you be more understanding of others' actions and attitudes. Proverbs 4:7 says, "Wisdom is the principle thing; therefore get wisdom; and in all thy getting, get understanding."

Some – The Negation of – All

"What we can or cannot do, what we consider possible or impossible, is rarely a function of our true capability. It is more likely a function of our beliefs about who we are."

- Anthony Robbins

Evangelist Freeman – reporting for duty! During my course work for my associate's degree in computer applications technology and my bachelor's degree in business, I had the opportunity to learn logic – the AND, OR, NOT functions. I had several classes where these principles were drilled into my brain. I will not expound on the AND, OR functions today – we will revisit those at another time. Today I want to focus on the NOT function in this article – negation. Negation, "indicates the opposite, usually employing the word not." So in my classes we were taught the NOT function using examples such as, "Today is Monday" versus "Today is not Monday." I said to myself, "This is easy." Well, it got a bit trickier as we progressed. When we were told to negate the word "All," I thought it would be "None." I was wrong. The negation of ALL is SOME. So, if we had a sentence that said "<u>All</u> mathematic problems <u>are</u> easy" the negation of that sentence would be "Some mathematatic problems are not easy." That is the rule for negating ALL – get it?

Now you may be saying, "Okay, Evangelist Freeman, where are you going with this?" I'm glad you asked. Satan is a liar and this fact is documented in John 8:44. God says He is the way the truth and the life – John 14:6. God also says that He is not a man that He should lie – Numbers 23:19. I heard someone say, "If God says my shirt is blue and it's green, the shirt would instantly turn blue because God cannot lie." If God speaks truth and Satan speaks lie, then Satan's job is to negate the Word of God by trying to convince you to believe the opposite of what God says. The enemy knows that if you believe and operate in the truth, he cannot "kill, steal, and destroy" in your life. So, let's examine a few ways He negates the word "ALL" in the Bible.

The Bible says in Philippians 4:13, "I can do all things through Christ which strengtheneth me." So in order to use the negation principle to make this point, understand that Philippians 4:13 is saying, "All things are doable through Christ which strengtheneth..." The negation of that verse is "Some things are not doable through Christ which strengtheneth..." The enemy is not trying to make you believe that you can do

NOTHING through Christ who strengthens you. Nothing is not the opposite of "ALL things ARE." The opposite of "ALL things ARE" is "SOME things are NOT." Satan knows how to negate the Word – remember, he's a liar. He knows you have too much evidence of things you were able to do through Christ who strengthened you. He tries to convince you that the new thing God is requiring of you is not doable. Those other things you did through Christ were doable but the new thing God is telling you to do is another story – ALL versus SOME. The enemy is saying, "Yea, you stopped using drugs but you cannot stop smoking cigarettes." The enemy is saying, "Yea, you got a GED, but you cannot complete college." If you feel fear, doubt, or unbelief about anything God is telling you to do – Satan is negating the Word. Your challenge is to stand on the Word that says, "ALL things ARE doable." God would not ask you to do something He is unable or unwilling to strengthen you to do.

Another example of the ALL versus SOME is found in Romans 8:28, "And we know that all things work together for good to them that love God, to them who are the called according to his purpose." So that verse is saying, "All things are working together for the good." Understand that this verse is addressed to those who love God and are called according to

His purpose. Satan wants you to believe that "Some things are not working together for your good" despite the fact that you love God and are called according to His purpose. He cannot convince you that NOTHING will work together for your good – you have too much evidence of things that God turned around for your good even though it looked impossible. The enemy is trying to convince you that the new challenge you are facing, this new dilemma, is not going to work out for your good. The enemy is saying, "Yea, God worked those other situations out so that they helped you instead of hurt you, but this one....OH BOY...this situation is something different and belongs in the "some are not" category." Don't believe the hype. I cannot tell you how many times Satan told me it was a wrap when I was on the streets. He tried to convince me to end it because there was no way out and there certainly was no way God could turn my pitiful, excuse of a life around and get something good out of it. Well, as Bishop Abney would say, "Look at God!" If he can flip the script on a crack cocaine addiction, what are you facing that the enemy is trying to convince you that God cannot do in your life? ALL versus SOME...that's the challenge...who will you believe! When the enemy tries to tell me how things are not going to work out for me, I remind him of how things are going to turn out for him. Revelations 20:10 says, "And the devil that deceived them was cast into the lake of fire and brimstone, where the beast and the false prophet are, and shall be tormented day and night for ever and ever." Yea, devil...it doesn't look too good for you and you can take that to the bank! Now, who should be worrying are how things are going to turn out?

My Issues Make My Budget and My Schedule

"The future is something which everyone reaches at the rate of 60 minutes an hour, whatever he does, whoever he is."

- C. S. Lewis

One of the groups that I do in my cognitive restructuring and resocialization program the *Lies That Bind®* is entitled "My Issues Make My Budget and My Schedule." Another group that usually precedes this group is entitled "Time and Energy – The Dynamic Duo." The purpose of these groups is to assist the group members in identifying the unconscious lies housed in their right brain that make decisions for them as it relates to their money, time, and energy without their conscious awareness. For the purpose of this article, we will group time and energy together because whatever one is doing with their time they are also utilizing energy.

According to experts in the fields of neuroscience and psychology, (Joseph, 1999 & Smith, 2000), positive and/or negative unconscious beliefs are implanted in the unconscious mind by what people observe and how they are treated during the formative years. If a person was raised in a situation in which they had to assume the responsibilities of others simply because they had no choice, that person may have internalized the lie, "I have to assume the responsibilities of others – I have no choice." As an adult, that individual may still find himself or herself obeying the directives of that lie which is now making their budget and their schedule. Say the person afflicted with this lie has a dream or a calling that necessitates they attend college to obtain credentials in order to enter a particular sphere of influence to affect change (salt and light change). If that person spends hours upon hours assuming the responsibilities of other perfectly capable adults, their destiny and purpose may be sitting on the backburner wondering if and/or when they will allocate some time, money, and energy into its fulfillment. It's hard to attend college classes, purchase textbooks, and study for exams when one is bailing people out of jail, picking someone up (who could have caught a bus), and babysitting for their adult children while they go to the club – AGAIN.

The same principle applies for other lies. Say a person is afflicted with the lie "You have to accept abuse without question." That person may spend hours (time) at the emergency room. After they leave the emergency room, they have to go to the drugstore (time) to fill the prescription (money) and buy makeup to cover the black-eye (money). They then have to go home and clean up the glass (time) and broken furniture, which will have to be replaced (money). That time could have been spent at the gym, or in a classroom, or reading a chapter in a textbook, or giving one's child a tour of a university campus. That money could have been spent on a software upgrade for one's computer, or a gym membership, or purchasing textbooks, or taking one's child to lunch and a movie.

In the end, it boils down to a contest, the lies versus purpose and destiny. Both are asking you to call the play – continue to obey the directives of lies or classify the lie for the thief it is and make a budget and schedule based on the truth. "The price of anything is the amount of life you exchange for it" - Henry David Thoreau

Finish Strong – The Homestretch

"The cost of regret far exceeds the price of discipline"

- Peter Lowe

This column is dedicated to students whether you are in high school or college. I am in the last semester of my second Master's degree. My body and mind are screaming for relief. There is something inside of me saying, "Ah, come on – give it a rest, Lady" but then there is the other voice saying, "FINISH STRONG!" Many of the motivational, inspirational sayings that I have programmed into my brain I learned at the gym. There was a class at the gym they called "G-Force." It is an extreme spin class. The regular spin class is tough but "G-Force" pushed the limits to the maximum. One of the things the instructor would say is "FINISH STRONG" when we were in the homestretch of the class. Some of the other sayings were: "It's all mental now, your body shut down 20 minutes ago. I know you are not going to let this machine beat you! Push through it!" Another voice I have in my head is Billy Blanks who would often say on his workout DVDs, "If you have to scream, SCREAM, but get through this workout!"

All my fellow students who are feeling the strain – PUSH THROUGH IT, FINISH STRONG, KEEP GOING, YOU GOT THIS, YOU CAN DO THIS, IF YOU HAVE TO SCREAM – SCREAM BUT GET THROUGH THIS WORKOUT! A point I think is good to make that I do not often hear motivational speakers articulate is – take care of yourself while you PUSH. It is important to eat healthy, exercise, and get some sleep. I know that sleep deprivation goes with the process of school, but know your limits. There are times when my body has said, "I refuse to take this abuse anymore – either get some rest or I'm shutting down." Based on experiences when my body refused to cooperate, I learned how to rest when I needed to and how to pace myself.

This homestretch is often the hardest part of the journey. If you have been going strong for a LONG time there is a part of you that may feel as if it deserves to slack off in the last quarter. Now is not the time to back down on the quality of your work – finish strong. Another thing the instructor says in "G-Force" spin is "FIND A WAY!" He was challenging us to find a way to make it to the finish line. During this last semester, there are times when I have to lay it down at 10:00 PM before I past out but that means I am up at 2:00 AM getting it in. I remember Bishop Noel Jones saying, "I will not speak slow down, I will not speak tired. If I have to crawl across the finish line..." I can hear Dr. Cindy Trimm saying, "The enemy wants to make you think you are tired of this and you are tired of that – AINT NOBODY TIRED BUT THE DEVIL! He's tired of your perseverance, he's tired of you refusing to give up!"

To my people in the homestretch – whether it's the homestretch of your first semester or the homestretch of your last semester – FINISH STRONG! Find a way; don't let a syllabus beat you! Refuse to give up! Take one for the team! Break the curse of poverty and lack. You can do this. If you have to take a nap – take a nap. If you have to pull back for a day, rest and regroup – then pull back, rest, regroup – then HIT IT HARD! You got this! I believe in you. Your destiny is on the other side of this pain. Your ancestors are looking over the balcony of heaven cheering for you. You can do this! When you walk across the stage – I will be with you in spirit. I'm walking across the stage this April. My sponsor from my 12-Step Program is walking across the stage this spring, and she did it on a walker due to an illness. Come on now...there are people in wheelchairs rolling across the stage this spring. I believe in you, and I believe in me! SMASH any obstacles that get in your path! You have come too far to turn back now! There is no greater feeling than when you lay that last paper or test on the desk on the last day. Cabbage patch all the way out the door – ah, you don't remember the cabbage patch dance☺. It's going down! See you on the stage! Do not worry about the "haters" in this last lap - who want what you are going after but do not want to do the work to get it. As Grete Waitz says, "For every finish-line tape a runner breaks - complete with the cheers of the crowd and the clicking of hundreds of cameras - there are the hours of hard and often lonely work that rarely gets talked about." I know the price you are paying and I salute you! Salute yourself in the mirror on your way out the door and – FINISH STRONG!

My Pain – My Purpose

"We delight in the beauty of the butterfly but rarely admit the changes it has gone through to achieve that beauty."

- Maya Angelou

Recently I had the honor of being the plenary speaker at a conference. I was asked to tell my story in order to communicate the message that restoration is possible no matter how incorrigible a person may appear. Later in the day when we were eating lunch, one well-meaning woman (I can read people pretty well) made a statement to me. She said, "We were so moved by your story, and we are so glad we didn't have your life." I smiled but I did not answer. At that point, even though I intellectually understood that she was trying to give me a compliment in the best way she could, I may have reacted emotionally with some "Dig this here." What I would have said if I was able to respond appropriately at that time was, "Every day of my life has contributed to my assignment on this earth. The only regret I have is the negative affect my life has had on those I love and my community for which I am making amends today." My purpose is connected to my pain.

Many people envy the ministry of others, but they do not envy the process. For example, I am anointed for psychological warfare. They call me "The Locksmith." I make keys for locks (mental locks), but that also means that I spent the first 12 years of my life in a torture chamber simultaneously experiencing the locks and keys. I was physically, mentally, sexually, verbally, and spiritually abused while learning the Word of God. Was that painful – YES! Did those experiences have a devastating affect on my life – YES! Did God take what was meant for evil and use it for my good – YES!

My life today is God's way of turning lemons into lemonade for His glory. He is using my pain to fuel my passion to help those who have been "locked up" in their minds. In order for my pain to be used in a beneficial manner for myself and society, I had to deny myself and pick up my cross and follow Christ. Meaning, I had to deny myself by denying my right to my anonymity when God told me that He wanted me to tell my story publicly. I had to pick up my cross: the stigma of my past, condescending looks, people who challenge my ministry due to my past, years of studying and writing papers, being ostracized for challenging the status quo, and so forth. Although there is a price to my purpose, there is nothing more beautiful and satisfying as when I see the level of freedom that those I work with experience by using the Keys of the Kingdom that God has given me to unlock the mind.

Whatever your purpose is on this earth can be connected to your pain. If you are asking God to reveal your purpose to you – your Kingdom Assignment, He will show you in time – keep asking. If you want a clue while you are waiting – it's connected to your pain. What hurt you? What makes you angry? What do you wish someone would do something about? That someone is probably you! I remember the day I discovered my Kingdom Assignment. Please allow me to share that beautiful experience with you.

I was doing a group for some of my court-mandated clients. I had them write down all the derogatory things people called them in their childhood on a piece of paper. I then had them write down all the derogatory things that people called them as adults. I recorded the labels people assigned them in their childhood on a tape recorder, and then I recorded the labels put on them as adults. My purpose for this group was to demonstrate to them that they were unconsciously doing an adult reenactment of their childhood script; but God had another plan. He hijacked my group in order to tell me what I was put on this earth to do. I played the tape, and while the derogatory names played loudly in the background, I walked back and forth in the room saying, "These messages are what cause us to make bad decisions: using drugs, losing our children, working the street, etc. When the messages stopped, I rewound the tape and played them again. I said, "We keep making bad decisions because these messages keep playing over and over and over in our head." The women were crying. I was crying...yes I was crying right with them. I had no plan for how to end the group. I guess I was just going to traumatize everyone and say, "That's all for today." God had a different plan – Whew! The Holy Spirit took over at that point because He knew I had reached the end of my bright idea. He asked the women through me, "What are we going to do? How are we going to stop these messages from playing over and over and over so we can stop doing the same destructive things over and over and over?" I looked at the tape recorder, and I said, "There is no erase button! There is a rewind button, but there is no erase button! How do we stop the messages?" One of the women in my group ran to the front of the room, looked me in my eye, and said, "Ms. Freeman, I know how we can make the messages stop. We can rewind the tape all the way to the beginning where the messages first start, and we can record something different over them." I then welcomed the women to the process of extracting lies and recording the truth.

Jesus said, "My sheep know my voice." God used one of the women I was assigned to help to tell me what my purpose on this earth was – my pain was given meaning that day! That was in 2003. That is what I do today. I am anointed to minister to the severely wounded. I take people back to their childhood where the life destroying messages were first recorded in their unconscious mind, we extract the lies, and we record something different over them – THE TRUTH. And ye shall know the truth, and the truth shall set you free! If the truth will set you free, it must be a lie that has you bound. MY PAIN = MY PURPOSE. My program – The *Lies That Bind®* is my purpose – MY KINGDOM ASSIGNMENT. Victor Frankl explained the pain and purpose equation so eloquently when he said, "What is to give light must endure burning." Ye are the light of the world!

Other Sheep – Not of This Fold...

"And I have other sheep [beside these] that are not of this fold. I must bring and impel those also; and they will listen to My voice and heed My call, and so there will be [they will become] one flock under one Shepherd"

- John 10:16 – AMP

Evangelist Freeman – reporting for duty. God gave me a special rhema revelation about John 10:16. For those unfamiliar with the term "rhema" it is defined as, "A verse or portion of Scripture that the Holy Spirit brings to our attention with application to a current situation or need for direction." In the context of the day when John 10:16 was written, Jesus was referring to gentiles when He said other sheep – of which we all qualify unless we are Jewish. A current situation that this verse can apply to in our day and time is the attitudes of certain people in the Body of Christ about the people from various subcultures that God is bringing into the church – for such a time as this. These people are walking away from dope houses, strip clubs, prisons, and various other less than savory places. Some of these people speak fluent profanity. Some of these people are completely "unchurched" – meaning they have not gone to church at all at any point in time. Many of these people are not dressed appropriately by society's standards. Some of these people do not know "church etiquette," and some may not understand spiritual authority and protocol. The revelation that God gave me was that He foreknew these people, and He predestined these people to <u>be conformed</u> (which is a process) into the image of His Son. Meaning: God didn't make the "other sheep" get saved; He simply knew that on a specific day at a specific time they would "call the play" and walk away from a life of sin, give their lives to Christ, and work for the Kingdom of God. Now, this may seem obvious to some, as we know we serve an omniscient God who so loved the world; but let me explain why I believe God gave me this revelation and why I am writing about this topic.

Many "saints" turn their nose up at certain people because of their backgrounds. They act as if there is a certain "church pedigree" that makes certain people more "usable" or "qualified" than "other sheep." This is not only my personal experience, I have spoken to many people who I know from other venues – besides the church – who have left certain lifestyles but do not come to church. I often ask them why and they tell me – because of how people, who know their history, look at them and treat them when they come to church. I have also heard people say "You couldn't handle my testimony." My thought to this statement is – REALLY – why couldn't someone handle your testimony – for heaven's sake! Some individuals have told me that I did not have to keep telling people where God brought me from as if my testimony makes people uncomfortable. Well, the way I look at it – some people's lack of a testimony makes me uncomfortable. God hasn't delivered their "deceitfully wicked heart" from anything? The Bible says, "For all have sinned...," it also says, "The heart is deceitfully wicked above all things..." The Bible didn't say the drug dealer has sinned and come short or the prostitute's heart is deceitfully wicked. Brothers and sisters – the Bible lumped us all together. The Bible also says, "But we are **all** as an unclean thing, and all our righteousnesses are as filthy rags..." Do we need to break down filthy rag? So that means our "best" behavior does not qualify us. For it is by grace are we saved and not of works lest any man should boast. So help me understand why Anneshia Freeman, or anyone else God delivered from a satanically designed trap, should be ashamed to tell people of the delivering power of God??? The Bible says they overcame by the blood of the Lamb and by the word of their testimony.

When I was in the crack house, God knew then that on August 7, 2000 when He would give me the ultimatum, "Choose you this day who you will serve" that I would walk away from that lifestyle and rededicate my life to Christ. Since God foreknew about August 7, 2000, He covered me, protected me (to a certain degree), and gave me revelations while I was in the "devil's camp" that would be applicable to my ministry today. On certain days when I was in the crackhouse, I would make jokes, and I would hear God, in my spirit, say, "The people who laugh are my sheep." The jokes I told, in hindsight, were "keys" (truths) that challenged the lies we were living at that time. "My sheep know my voice." The people who did not laugh, God let me know in my spirit, were goats. Some people did not find anything I said the least bit funny and promptly said, "Shut up crackhead – you talk too much!" God gave all sorts of parables in the Bible to help "churchy folks" sort through their beliefs and feelings related to God, giving family rights to people who just entered the fold. The parable of the workers in the vineyard found in Matthew 20:1-16 addresses this issue. The workers who agreed to certain terms and conditions for employment in this particular vineyard were upset because the vineyard owner hired some people at the last hour and paid them the same wage. Can you see the application to this "other sheep" issue? Then we have the parable of the prodigal son. I was raised in the church but ended up on the streets. Then I came back home. That is the case with many of the "other sheep." God also said, "I'll have mercy on who I want to have mercy (Romans 9:15 -16)." The Kingdom is a theocracy. God makes "family selection" decisions all by Himself!

Another point I feel is very important about "other sheep," is that Satan does not waste resources. If he took the time and effort to "bind" someone up so tight that they are "tied" to the dope-house, a prison cell, or a bar stool, then he must really be intimidated by the gifts and callings on their lives. He cannot touch what God put in them so he had to mess their minds up so badly that they cannot operate in their gifts for the Kingdom of God. So when you see a girl standing on a corner in a miniskirt and fishnet stockings or when you see a young man being put in the back of a police car for selling drugs, a good question to ask yourself would be, "I wonder what gifts they have that so intimidates Satan that he "tied" them up that tight?" Now the role of mature children of God is to be ready for the "other sheep" when they enter the fold, "In the last days I will pour out my spirit on all flesh." When Jesus raised Lazarus from the dead, He told the people standing around to untie him. That is our job! The church is supposed to "untie/loose" people from the lies of Satan and "tie-up/bind" the works of the devil in the earth realm. I would like to thank the people that God has used over the past 12 years to "untie" me. Thank you for doing as you have been commanded. If you do not have a Titus 2:3-4 ministry in your church – think about getting one. To the people with the proud looks who turn their nose up at the "other sheep," check out Proverbs 6:17 and Proverbs 21:4.

Now, let us end with a word to the "other sheep." Don't be a punk. No one ran you out the club or the dope house. Why would you allow someone to run you out the church? As long as the leadership welcomes you and treats you as one of the fold, then ignore the white-washed tombs full of dead men's bones. Now if the leadership is turning their nose up, you might want to find another church. Do not get discouraged and give up. Did you give up if you were trying to find some dope, and the first dope man didn't have what you were looking for?

Ask God to direct you to the fold where your earthly shepherd will care for you so he can teach you about your Heavenly Shepherd. Listen to instructions like you listened to instructions at the dope house and in prison. Sanctification is a process, and we all need to be purified in the refiner's fire. Stay connected to the Body so you can be fed.

One last word to the "other sheep." Do not run out to the battlefield poorly trained for battle. We are a part of the "Joshua Generation." We have fire in our blood, but we need our "generals" to teach us how to fight – the weapons are not carnal. You do not have to feel inferior to anyone in the Body of Christ. Remember what Jesus said to you in John 15:16, "You have not chosen Me, but I have chosen you and I have appointed you [I have planted you], that you might go and bear fruit and keep on bearing, and that your fruit may be lasting [that it may remain, abide], so that whatever you ask the Father in My Name [as presenting all that I Am], He may give it to you." Word, to my "other sheep" folks!

Learning the Hard Way – Is That Really Necessary?

"Human beings, who are almost unique in having the ability to learn from the experience of others, are also remarkable for their apparent disinclination to do so."

- Douglas Adams

How many times have you heard someone exclaim, "I finally learned my lesson" or something similar like, "I bumped my head a thousand times before I finally figured it out." Does every life lesson have to be learned at the "school of hard knocks?" Many individuals have been conditioned by the learning styles they witnessed and experienced during their formative years. They have internalized those methodologies as the only valid way to gain knowledge.

If a child is raised in an environment in which he/she witnessed others around them making the same self-destructive decisions repeatedly until something tragic happened, that child internalized that process. If a child was left to his/her own devices to figure out things on their own that they should have been taught, that child internalized that process as a learning style. According to Dr. Ed Smith, noted Christian psychologist, parents and other adults are teaching children whether they know it or not, "WHATEVER I tell them through my actions and words will be the truth for them, even if it is a lie" (Smith, 2000). Parents can teach their children how not to learn as well as how to learn.

Later when that child has grown into adulthood, he/she is still unconsciously thinking and acting as a child. Meaning: there may be several learning methods available to that person, but their unconscious belief system will tell them that they are not eligible to learn in that particular way. He/She will choose the hard, painful way that they have been programmed to think is normal. For example, there are times when I have witnessed certain people about to make mistakes that I knew would cost them dearly, because I have made those same mistakes in the past. So I shared the lessons I learned with them. It is not as if I am talking about people who had to wonder if they could trust me or if my motives were right. I am talking about individuals who would declare with no hesitation that they know I have their best interest at heart. Those same people smiled and nodded agreeably to my advice and went and jumped off the same cliff I warned them about SEVERAL TIMES and ended up in a full body cast. When I visited them in the hospital...I mean the jail... I mean the prison...I mean the rehab center...they looked me in the eye and declared, "Well I learned my lesson this time!" The fact of the matter is that they learned THAT particular lesson...the hard way...that particular time. Unfortunately, the next time they need information, instead of reading a book to gain that knowledge, or talking to someone who has information in that area, or going to a seminar... their unconscious belief system will tell them they MUST once again sign up for a class at the "Hard Way University."

I am not judging people who are afflicted with that self-defeating learning style. I only recognize it so well because that was my learning style most of my life until it was exposed. "And ye shall know the truth and the truth will set you free." The truth is: YOU DO NOT HAVE TO LEARN <u>EVERYTHING</u> THE HARD WAY. Yes, there will be times that you have to experience painful lessons, but that should be a last resort lesson plan that is not left up to you to select. If you know you need some information in a particular area, PLEASE find a softer, easier way to learn. One of my undergrad professors said something very powerful one day in class, "Whether the process is painful or not is irrelevant to the result." If you can learn about the law of gravity from a book or sitting at the feet of a wise scholar, does it really matter that you have the same information as someone that jumped off a cliff fifty times to acquire the same knowledge? You can ask, learn, and implement while others are suffering at the "school of hard knocks."

Why Are You So Fearful…
How Is It That You Have No Faith?

"You can discover what your enemy fears most by observing the means he uses to frighten you."

- Eric Hoffer

I have my Evangelist hat on again this week. One evening last year, I decided to put my books and papers aside and go to a church I had been watching on television for a while to see a particular pastor. I was upset to learn that he would not be there that evening and was about to leave when the Holy Spirit said "Sit down." So guess what I did? I sat down. I received several nuggets, but I did not get the Word that I felt I was there to get until close to the end of the service when the minister said something very simple –but it has changed my life. This minister from African said, "There are 66 books in the Bible. The only part of the Bible that will work for you is the part you believe!" WRGO readers, I made a decision that day. The decision I made was that if I was going to do this "Kingdom of God" thing, I might as well believe everything the Word says. Now some may say, "Duh…come on Evangelist Freeman – isn't that the point anyway?" Well let me challenge you by asking you a couple questions, "Does your life reflect that you have internalized everything the Bible says? Does your life, attitudes, and decisions reflect that you believe everything written in all 66 books?" Okay, now that we have determined that Anneshia isn't the only one who can quote the Bible but needs a deeper revelation on certain principles contained in the scriptures, let's move on.

Today I want to attack the spirit of fear. That's right – let's whip some devil tail today. The quote I began the column with by Eric Hoffer says a lot. It says that your enemy reveals what they fear about you by the means they use to frighten you. Well, my thought is that Satan reveals what his greatest weapons are by what he uses the most to try to stop people. In my life, and the lives of many others, he has used lies that produce fear. So, lies and fear – from what I can see – are Satan's two main weapons. Therefore, the two most powerful weapons for spiritual warfare are the truth and faith. So for the rest of the article allow me to share some truths with you from the Word of God to attack fear.

First, Matthew 28:18 says, "And Jesus came and spoke unto them saying, all authority is given unto me in heaven and in earth." If I believe that – REALLY believe that – then what shall I fear? Proverbs 18:10 say, "The name of the Lord is a strong tower; the righteous runneth into it and is safe." Now if I believe that – REALLY believe that, then I know I can call on the name of the Lord when trouble arises, and I am SAFE (said with the sign used for "safe" in a baseball game). Psalms 62:11 says, "God has spoken once, twice have I heard this, that power belongeth unto God." Then if I look over in Luke 10:19 in the Amplified Bible it says, "Behold! I have given you authority and power to trample upon serpents and scorpions, and [physical and mental strength and ability] over all the power that the enemy [possesses]; and NOTHING shall in any way harm you." Hey, if I truly believe that power belongs to God and that he has given me power over the enemy...then why does fear try to creep in because a few uncircumcised Philistines are threatening me?

Okay, this is getting good. Let's be a little more specific in the attack on the spirit of fear. First, let's clarify that fear is a spirit, and it is not of God. It plainly states in II Timothy 1:7, "For God hath not given us the spirit of fear; but of power, and of love, and of a sound mind." That being the case, then why does Satan try to make us afraid at times because a few people are plotting on us? Satan has a way of letting you know he got some agents plotting – right. The answers for the plots are in the Word also. In Proverbs 21:30 (Amplified Bible) it says, "There is no [human] wisdom or understanding or counsel [that can prevail] against the Lord." In addition, Proverbs 15:3 says, "The eyes of the Lord are in every place, keeping watch on the evil and the good." God is at your enemies' committee meetings. He also says in Psalm 33:16 (Amplified Bible) "No king is saved by the great size and power of his army; a mighty man is not delivered by [his] much strength." One more punch – right in the face of the devil. The Word says in Isaiah 54:17, "No weapon that is formed against thee shall prosper, and every tongue that shall rise against you in judgment thou shall condemn. This is the <u>heritage</u> of the servants of the Lord, and their righteousness is from me, saith the Lord." The same Lord who has all power saith this unto thee!!!

Let me finish by saying that you can believe what God says because of Numbers 23:19, "God is not a man that He should lie; neither the son of man that He should repent; hath He said; and shall He not do it? Or hath He spoken and shall he not make it good?" If God said He's got your back – He's got your back. He does not NEED you or me, so He doesn't have to lie to us to get us to be with Him. He loves us and guess what, I

John 4:18 says, "There is no fear in love, but perfect love casteth out fear, because fear hath torment. He that feareth is not made perfect in love." We can now understand that a lie is the negation of the truth. When Satan tries to bring fear into our lives, he is saying the Word is lying to you. Choose you this day, who you will believe – the father of lies or the truth – Jesus said "I am the way, the Truth..."

I will end with a quote by Marcus Aurelius, "If you are distressed by anything external, the pain is not due to the thing itself, but to your estimate of it; and this you have the power to revoke at any moment."

Our Father, Which Art...The Missing File

"My father? I never knew him.
Never even seen a picture of him."

- Eminem

Today I have my Evangelist hat on. I want to share with you a revelation that God has been sharing with me lately. I am going to speak in the first person throughout this article but this is written for every person who struggles with the concept...Our Father. This article is addressed to people who have some unaddressed issues with the authority figures who raised them and have a hard time conceptualizing God as a Father – on a deep level.

God has been showing me that not only do I need to be healed from the lies that Satan planted in my unconscious mind about myself and my relationships with people; God has been showing me how the lies affect my relationship with Him. My struggle has been with internalizing the concept of an authority figure that loves me unconditionally, that protects me, that provides for me, who has a good plan for my life and the resources to make that plan a reality. I know the Word. I can quote the Word. I challenge stimuli thrown my way by "the agents" with the Word. I have internalized many principles contained in the Word, but God has been showing me that I still struggle with internalizing the love of God. Why, because of a missing file and a distorted file in my unconscious mind...it's the "When I Was a Child...Syndrome."

Joseph (1992), noted expert in the fields of neuroscience and psychology, states, "The mind of the child is malleable. Impressions are easily made and maintained. Indeed, just as an impression of someone's hand can be left in wet cement, the impressions made by our parents also make an impression in the very malleable, as yet unformed psyche of the child. These linked impressions stay with us forever in the form of an internalized Parent, which continues to exert influences similar to those exerted by our parents, but within the confines of our own psyche" (p. 175). Dr. Joseph goes on to explain that, "...future thoughts, feelings, fears, hopes, and desires will echo the feelings, descriptions, pronouncements, and images repeatedly imposed on us by our parents" (p. 175). This would be a good thing if the feelings, descriptions, pronouncements, and images repeatedly imposed on us by our parents were loving, caring, inspirational, and in line with what the Word says about us. According to Joseph, if we were repeatedly told we were failures, "...the parental voice will echo forever in the form of a Parent Ego personality that is now inside us" (p. 175). That is...until that voice is reprogrammed with a revelatory understanding of the Word of God.

My therapist☺, Dr. R. Joseph (1992), also defined the unconscious child. He states, "Although as adults we have grown, matured, had new experiences, assumed new responsibilities, changed our minds over a thousand times, and done and said things we swore we never would, the Child at our central core remains the child it always was. This Child continues to harbor the same feelings, emotions, resentments, frustrations, and memories that were present during childhood" (p. 166). Now this is the part that made me do a backwards flip and throw the book across the room, "If this Child was rejected or abused, it continues to feel and act as if it were being rejected and abused long after we have attained adulthood. If it was predominantly loved, praised, encouraged, and treated with dignity and respect, it continues to expect such treatment long after we have become adults. How we were raised and the environmental stresses and parental pressures we experienced not only shaped the character of the Child but continue to exert formidable influences on how we behave and interact as adults. Indeed, sometimes, the Child never grows up and remains fixated in the character at a certain traumatic point in life" (p. 166-167). So, according to this expert, we have a part in our brain that has the personality characteristics of the people of influence from our childhood (unconscious parent) that continues to exert the same powerful influences exerted on us by the authority figures who raised us. In addition, we have a part of our brain (unconscious child) that continues to respond to the parental dictates in the same way we responded as a child…it's the "When I Was a Child Syndrome."

So, when I was a child, there were certain dynamics going on between me and the authority figures in my life. Now as I describe the authority figures that raised me, please understand that I am not judging them; I am simply stating the facts. I now know that what I experienced as a child was a generation curse, and the people who hurt me were hurt by their primary caretakers and so forth. When I was a child, the authority figures in my life were mean, demanding, insensitive to my needs, untrustworthy, nitpicky perfectionist, selfish, irresponsible, controlling, extremely judgmental, and so forth. That was when I was a child. The authority figures called me names, put unrealistic expectations on me, punished me for the slightest infraction, and so forth. That was when I was a child. As a child, I received validation only when I performed perfectly and the moment the performance ended, I was expected to perform again, and again, and again. That happened...when I was a child. Now, let's bring all these concepts together with my topic...Our Father...the missing file.

God has been revealing my current struggle – reprogramming my unconscious parent and unconscious child file with the truth. If I had grown up in an environment where I was protected by authority figures instead of injured by them, it would be easy to internalize the concept of God as a protector. God revealed his ability to protect me when I was using drugs. That's right – when I was lost in sin, God protected me. Come on now, I was out there everyday when that man killed 17 girls in Detroit. He protected me so well that drug dealers were afraid of me because every time they did something to me or tried to do something to me, something bad happened to them or someone close to them. So why do I still at times struggle with the concept of a Father who protects his children. Lord help us...help us know you in the power of your might. Help us wounded people heal and know that you love us and that you got our backs. Help us understand that if you are omnipotent, and we are your children, that we should "fear no evil for thou art with us."

As a child, the love I received was conditional. If I had received unconditional love, I would not struggle so much with the concept of God's unconditional love. I would not struggle so much with watching God protect those who belong to Him who are messing up big time when I feel as if I am doing so well. Snap out of it Anneshia. Don't get amnesia. God help us internalize the concept of your unconditional love. Help us understand that you love us whether we perform perfectly or if we mess up. Help us also understand that when you chastise us that it is a form of love and that you are doing it to help us be better. Help us understand that if you wanted to kill us you could have done that a long time ago. Help us internalize the fact that you love us where we are right now in the process of sanctification and that "He which hath a begun a good work in us will perform it..."

Another issue I struggle with is Our Father as a provider. When I was a child, my authority figures were poor – poor and irresponsible. So even the little money that came into the household was not used appropriately.

Therefore, my needs often went unmet. I watched others have while I suffered lack. The derivative effect was the "I'm going to get my hustle on…I got this…I going to get mine…You get yours" mentality. Now as an adult, although I know I have to do my part because faith without works is dead, I still struggle with understanding on a deep level that God is a loving Father and all the silver and gold belong to Him. God help us understand that you are our provider. Help us who were let down so many times by those who were supposed to provide for us internalize that you delight in blessing your children. Help us understand that you will not give a gold watch to a two year old so as we grow and mature you will prosper us as our soul prospers. Help us understand that your love is unconditional but your blessings have conditions on them, which is also demonstrative of your love for us. Help us speak to these mountains of lack about Our Father and make them move. Help us God! Help us connect the experiences most of us have already had to the characteristics of a loving, caring, protective, nurturing, correcting, providing Father. Help us get to know you better. Friedrich Nietzische puts it this way, "Whoever does not have a good father should procure one." If we say God is Our Father, we have a good father. Lord, help us internalize this fact!

References

Joseph, R. (1992). *The right brain and the unconscious: Discovering the stranger within*. New York & London: Plenum Press.

Smith. E.(2000). *Beyond tolerable recovery.* Campbellsville, Kentucky: Family Care Publishing.